LEADERSHIP:

Theory and Practice to Become a Successful Leader to Guide and Motivate your Team in Companies, in Organizations, in Work, in Sport, in Life

Table of Contents

Introduction 4
Chapter One: Types of Leaders 7
Chapter Two: Effective Communication Strategies For Leaders 16
Chapter Three: Dealing With People 26
Chapter Four: Picking The Right People 37
Chapter Five: Characteristics To Develop as a Leader 44
Chapter Six: Building a Vision For Your Team or Followers 62
Chapter Seven: Consultation 68
For Decision Making 68
Chapter Eight: Develop the Confidence to Start Asking 72
Chapter Nine: Solid Tips For Increasing Your Influence Over People 80
Chapter Ten: Tips For Being a Leader Everyone Loves To Follow! 93
Chapter Eleven: Tips For Being an Effective Leader at Business Networking Events 99
Chapter Twelve: Tips For Boosting Your Charisma as a Leader 106
Conclusion 124

Introduction

Do you think leaders are special species born with extraordinary powers? Do you really believe leaders cannot be created or trained? Be honest. Do you think leadership skills are not something that can be acquired? Have you been living with a self-limiting belief that you do not have it in you to be a leader?

Well, to burst the bubble, anyone can be a leader if they are willing to develop specific characteristics that inspire faith in people. Teachers in schools are leaders. Managers in corporate organizations are leaders. Politicians are leaders. The leader qualities described in the book are universally applicable for anyone in a leadership position or aspiring to be in a leadership role.

Every group of people or institution needs a powerful leader to achieve their goals. There has to be someone to inform them, direct their actions and inspire them. Most importantly, there has to be someone the group of people can trust or have faith in. A leader needs to meet the expectations and obligations of his organization, community or country. He needs to duly discharge his duties and responsibilities towards people who have restored their faith in him to lead them.

When a powerful leadership is at the helm of affairs, success is inevitable. Similarly, when leadership crumbles, failure is almost certain. There are certain qualities a leader must possess. For starters, trust. People must be able to trust their decisions and have faith in their guidance.

Nelson Mandela was loved by people not because he was born in another cosmic universe with celestial powers. People loved him because they had complete faith in his abilities to empathize with them and transform their lives from the shackles of societal evil and injustice.

Leaders must be honest, ethical and fair in all management affairs. They must be able to safeguard property and people's rights. There must be a sense of transparency in handling financial obligations and focus on the safety of members.

The test of true leadership is not when followers are following you and it is all hunky dory. Real leadership does not come shining forth when everything is going great and things are in order. How does a true leader deal with people who are terribly disappointing him/her? Leaders show plenty of tact, mercy, gentleness and compassion. Being in a position of authority awards them with a sense of responsibility towards people, which doesn't necessarily mean being harsh, rugged or aggressive.

Leaders can be made. You can be an exceptional leader even if you are not convinced yet. You need to work with the right intention, enhance certain characteristics and emulate the example of successful leaders. Everyone has it in them to be a leader. We all deal with people on a daily basis. All of us have it in us to be leaders, yet only a few of us become great leaders. Why?

Because only a few are willing to fine tune their leadership skills. Only a few are ready to go that extra mile for becoming an inspiring leader. Only a few are willing to delay gratification and develop habits that will make them formidable leaders. Only a few will get rid of excuses and replace them with goals. Will you be one of them?

Get rid of procrastination by setting smaller milestones for big tasks rather than a single deadline. This way the task at hand doesn't seem humungous and you will be more on course with smaller milestones rather than beginning work a day before the huge project is to be completed. Avoid time killers like the social media or virtual games. Avoid the analysis paralysis that prevents you from accumulating information without acting on it. Just take the first step and everything else will follow. The right time is now. Give up excuses.

Chapter One: Types of Leaders

You've worked in different work environments, haven't you? While one boss may have been open to feedback and suggestions, another may have been an absolute tyrant, while still another may hardly be involved in decision-making. The vision and culture of various businesses often determine their leadership style. Each style has its own pros and cons, and depends on the organization's overall goals. Here's a heads up on some of the most common leadership styles to help you identify what works for you and your business goals.

Laissez Faire

These leaders are ideal for teams that are highly trained and accomplished, and can work under minimal supervision. The leader is not directly involved in supervising employees or providing regular feedback. It cannot be used for all employees though.

The Laissez faire leadership style can save time and help teams achieve multiple goals since the members are all highly skilled, efficient and motivated to work without guidance. However, research has pinned this down as one of the least effective leadership styles since it does not work well if the group does not possess sufficient knowledge or decision making skills.

Minimal supervision from leaders can lead to ineffectual production, little control and higher costs.

Steve Jobs and Warren Buffet perfectly represent the laissez faire leadership style. Jobs was known for communicating his vision to employees, giving them a goal to be achieved and subsequently letting them work without interference. If unhappy with the end result, he simply fired people entrusted with the task.

Warren Buffet is another shinning laissez faire example. He awards his employees complete freedom to handle projects and come up with innovative solutions for business problems. Buffet only gets involved in dire circumstances. He has attributed his business success to employing highly capable and original thinking individuals, who Buffet even good naturedly claims are much savvier than him.

Autocratic Leader

The autocratic leadership style centers absolute decision making power to the leader. This style is more hands-on leadership. The leader assigns orders, allocates tasks without much consultation and assumes complete responsibility or full authority of the functioning of the business. The leader imposes his will on the team, and makes decisions without being open to inputs or suggestions.

Autocratic or authoritative leadership style is ideal for people who need to work with clear directions in close supervision. Some businesses and projects may need a solid leader, who can get tasks done effectively and in time. However, the downside is creative and innovative thinking team members may detest this working style and feel more devalued or de-motivated. Hard boiled authoritative leaders may rely on negative reinforcement of penalty and fear for getting work done from employees in a more dogmatic manner. This is likely to increase resent, rebellion and low productivity. People can feel intimidated, bullied and controlled. Though it can be effective in guiding a new and inexperienced team, it doesn't work very well in an environment where the team possesses more expertise and experience than the leader.

Helen Gurley Brown, the former editor-in-chief of Cosmopolitan is much known for her authoritative leadership style, which helped her consistently publish content reflecting American values, and raking in steady profits for three decades. Brown was a tough task master who flourished in getting goals achieved with little scope for error.

Participative

As the name suggests, participative leadership is more democratic in nature. It encourages inputs from subordinates or team members, though the leader retains responsibility of making the final decision. It is helpful in business scenarios where people are capable of coming up with ideas but also need someone to be in charge of clear decision making.

Participative leaders believe in decentralizing authority. They often consult with team members and subordinates before formulating policies. Team members are actively involved in decision making, though the responsibility still rests with the leader. Participative leaders are often nothing more than moderators in a process involving brainstorming of ideas and suggestions. The group is lead by example, motivation and persuasion rather than force.

This leadership style can increase employee morale because they are an important part of the decision making process. Participative leadership can inspire greater commitment and involvement by employees. It is believed to grow the enthusiasm, motivation and co-operation of employees, resulting in lower absenteeism, reduced attrition, better performance and higher productivity. It may not work well in scenarios where employees do not possess sufficient knowledge, expertise or experience to contribute to a quality decision making process.

Jim Lentz, the Chief Executive Officer of Toyota Motor North America, Inc. is a fine example of participative leadership. He has guided the company's employees through challenges and minimized damage, while addressing important issues. He led from the front when several million units were recalled owing to faulty brakes, and motivated others to follow suit by pitching their own ideas and suggestions.

Consultative

This leadership style thrives on using the experiences, abilities and ideas of others for achieving a goal. However, the final decision making still rests with the leader. The style focuses more on consulting with folks who will be directly impacted by the decision. The decision is passed through members who are affected by it, before the leader takes a final call. Their inputs and suggestions are actively sought to make the implementation even more effective. Consultative leaders often involve subordinates and team members in the problem solving process, though they retain the final decision making. They are happy to delegate, but keep the veto power to weigh all options for arriving at the best decision, which is in everyone's interest.

Much like participative leaders, consultative leaders inspire a higher employee morale and improved efficiency. However, a more people oriented and less task oriented approach may not work where people are not expert or experienced enough to offer suggestions in matters that are directly related to them. They may need a more directed or controlled leader to lead them with the right expertise.

Transactional Leader

In transaction leaderships, team members receive instant and tangible rewards for implementing the leader's command. The leadership thrives on an exchange of benefits. It is a more structured and restricted approach where people are supposed to adhere to a certain way implementing orders. It is more observed in political settings and bureaucratic organizations. Team members receive either rewards or penalty depending on performance results corresponding to predetermined goals. All rewards and punishments for meeting objectives are clearly stated at the onset.

The advantage of this leadership style is that it motivates employees and makes them more productive, based on a clear reward and punishment model. It offers employees clearer short term goals and a higher sense of autonomy in the absence of micromanagement.

One of the biggest disadvantages of this leadership model is that it views motivation in a simplistic light, often failing to consider key individual differences. The style can involve greater rigidity of a pre worked out system, higher scope for passing the blame and a clear demarcation between leaders and employees. It puts the onus of accountability solely on workers and does not encourage creativity or lateral thinking.

Bill Gates is a prominent transactional leader. He would monitor new product teams and pose tough questions to workers until he was suitably convinced that the teams understood the company's vision and were on their way for an impressive performance.

Transformational Leader

Transformational leadership style relies heavily on intense communication from leaders for meeting goals. Leaders are constantly motivating employees and boosting productivity through greater visibility and efficiency. This leadership style involves greater involvement of the leader for meeting management goals. Leaders are focused on the larger picture and are open to delegating minor tasks for accomplishing a bigger goal.

Transformational leadership utilizes inspiration for motivating employees. It creates more enthusiasm, innovations and transformations. It encourages followers to work beyond their self interest, and can lead to greater productivity. Owing to a more proactive leadership, followers form greater expectations. Transformational leadership can create more leaders from among the followers.

Although it has its advantages, the leadership can backfire if the leader is a self serving, immoral or hatred inducing person like Osama Bin Laden or Adolf Hilter. Subordinates are often left to face the fire of decisions that have a negative impact or are not thoughtfully made. Another fallacy of this method is motivation is always assumed without taking changes into consideration.

Servant Leadership

Some leaders almost always place the needs of their followers before them. Their fundamental objective is to serve and safeguard the interests of followers. Though this type of leadership in more observed in public sectors than businesses, corporations can have better leaders by adopting the servant leadership style. The goal of good leaders should ideally be to serve their followers and keep their interests paramount.

This leadership style is based on the premise that the leader doesn't benefit as much from the leadership as his/her followers. Leaders act selflessly and with greater altruistic tendencies. The primary goal is service and not power. Moral authority for serving followers rather than wielding power should be the ideal goal of all leaders.

The model may not work well in a business environment though it can be an ideal leadership type. There may be a lack of authority, which can result in low motivation among employees or followers. It may feature a limited vision, and direct goals towards higher causes than profit making. This can be an advantage or disadvantage based on your corporate goals.

The advantages of this leadership style include greater loyalty, more employee involvement and higher productivity. Some of the world's most famous servant leaders are Nelson Mandela,

Mahatma Gandhi, Mother Teresa and Martin Luther King, Jr. These are people who assumed leadership to bring about change for the betterment of people in a selfless and altruistic manner.

Chapter Two: Effective Communication Strategies For Leaders

Successful business leaders need solid communication skills. This is probably one of the most fundamental traits that differentiate extraordinary leaders from dreary ones. Exceptionally good leaders are ones who have weaved communication skills into their leadership practices. Talk to any business scholar about the most basic trait of leadership skills, and chances are they'll cite communication skills. When two people have similar qualifications, education, knowledge, skills and experience, the one who bags the leader's role is someone who displays stellar communication competency. Here are some powerful communication tips to sharpen your leadership profile.

Do Not Use Derogatory Words

Effective leaders never pepper their speech with abusive language, swear words, cuss words or tawdriness. Instead they use language that is powerful, effective and meaningful. If your words and phrases are more beneficial, balanced and non-derogatory, people are likelier to listen to it.

For instance, instead of calling someone abusive names for not doing a job well, you could focus on how they are otherwise talented and how not performing well could jeopardize their high chances of growth and promotion.

Make the criticism meaningful and relevant to them rather than going on a personal swear word rant and revealing your true class in turn. Leaders are role models. They are people who are looked up to by followers. Stooping down to an abysmally low level doesn't do justice to a leader's stature. Talk in a mature, positive and harmonious way if you want followers to take note.

Always Speak The Truth

Leaders should not use their position unethically to accuse, blame or act with prejudice. They should be shining examples of honestly, integrity, ethics and fairness.

Dishonest and unscrupulous leaders do not inspire the faith of their followers for long. Hiding information, doctoring the truth and spreading false stories only tarnishes your image as a leader when the truth comes out.

Talk to People With Full Attention

Talk to people with rapt attention when you are having a face to face conversation. Be quiet. The lesser you talk; the more people listen to you. Attempt to listen to the other person before launching a talkathon. Focus on understanding the other person than being understood. Don't just listen to talk back; listen to understand what the other person is trying to convey.

Listening is as much a component of communication skills as talking. It helps you open your mind to newer ideas, perspectives and insights. It helps you learn something you may not already know. Display body language that facilitates people to share more with you. Keep an open demeanor. Do not cross your arms or legs. Let your palms be open. Always have a pleasant expression and positive countenance. Do not be pre occupied with your phone or other devices when you are talking to your employees or followers. It doesn't show seriousness for what you are talking. If you want them to listen with conviction, you must learn to talk with conviction.

Always communicate important messages face to face. It gives you the opportunity to observe non verbal clues of communication such as body language and facial expressions. The process of communication becomes much more effective when you combine verbal and non verbal communication channels.

Solicit Feedback

Though it isn't easy, soliciting feedback is important for leaders. Subordinates or team members may not feel too comfortable sharing an honest feedback with an authority. You need to create an atmosphere where people are freely able to break through apprehensions and honestly share their views. This may not always be flattering. You should be prepared to handle honest and genuine criticism.

Take your followers into confidence and tell them you make mistakes too like everyone else. They should point out those mistakes without feeling threatened, awkward or intimidated. Feedback and constructive criticism is essential for your growth. Be open to suggestions that will enhance your management practices, company goals and overall productivity. A good leader is always open to learning from followers without resorting to ego games.

Send Positive Messages

Encourage people all the time. It drives them to achieve even greater results when they know their efforts are acknowledged and appreciated. Studies reveal people who have a stronger sense of purpose tend to be more creative, tougher and focused. It never hurts to remind your workers or team members how they are changing people's lives. Certain research studies reveal how recognition and a sense of belonging are sometimes more important than salaries for increasing employee loyalty.

Give people greater responsibility. Nothing makes them feel as valued as when they are entrusted with important tasks. If they do not perform the task according to your expectation, avoid being harsh. Gently suggest the right way to do things or inform them tactfully how things like these can prolong the success they truly deserve.

Your words can leave behind permanent and damaging wounds. Therefore, always use positive, encouraging, inspiring, constructive and motivating words than harsh language and destructive criticism that tears apart people's morale.

Avoid Getting Angry

There was a small boy with a rather foul temper. His dad handed him a bag of nails and asked him to hammer a nail into the fence each time the boy lost his cool. The first day saw 37 nails being drilled into the fence by the boy. Gradually, the number of nails drilled into the fence reduced. The boy discovered he it was easier to just hold back his anger than go through the entire process of drilling nails into the fence.

One day the little boy did not lose his temper even once. He went and told his father proudly. The father then asked him to remove a nail for each day he was successful in holding his temper. Several days passed and the nails were now all gone. The father then held his hand and took him to the fence. He said, "You did it well son. However, look at the holes left behind. The fence can never be the same again. When you say things in a rage, they leave permanent scars behind. It doesn't matter how many times you feel or say sorry, the wound is forever."

It doesn't pay to be a modern day Adolf Hitler. Harsh reprimands may get people to perform out of fear in the short run. However, it will be least effective in the long run, owing to reduced team morale, low motivation, and a non-existent higher purpose for achieving the goal. Be patient and tolerant towards people's weaknesses. Rather than getting angry, see how you can help them overcome these shortcomings to boost productivity.

The famous Machiavellian quote comes to mind. "And here comes the question whether it is better to be loved rather than feared or feared rather than loved." While a balance of both is ideal, love may help you gain fierce loyalty, companionship and faith. It makes followers intrinsically motivated to put in their best to prevent letting their leader down. This can be far more potent than physical rewards or reprimand.

You may believe fear is more potent and stable when it comes to getting tasks done. However, it can also lead to corruption and unscrupulous means in which people try to bend the system to avoid reprimand. Rather than acting with a sense of internal loyalty, they are simply doing things to avoid punishment or the wrath of their leader, which may lead them to unethical means.

Take Adolf Hitler for instance. He was someone who led by nothing but fear. He rose to power quickly by instilling a sense of fear into his followers. People had little choice but to comply. What were the results? Devastating to say the least.

Body Language

Body language is an integral component of your persona as a leader. Your voice tone, expressions, gestures, walk, posture and several other non verbal clues are a clincher when it comes to conveying your leadership.

Always keep the tone of your voice assertive, firm, determined and low. Studies have revealed that talking to people in soothing and comforting low tones actually makes them more efficient. This is no way implies you shouldn't have a strong, assured and naturally confident voice that shows you mean business. Just do not go around talking in high tones all the time for the sake of asserting your authority if you want people to take you seriously. Always speak slowly and pause for effective to reinforce authority. You will appear less authoritative if you talk fast without peppering your speech with impactful pauses.

A leader's handshake is firm without being intimidating and tight. Your objective should be to assure people rather than establish a status quo with your handshake. Do not resort to a limp handshake by using only the finger tips of your hand. Use the entire hand. You get a single chance to create a powerful first impression, and your handshake can make an instant impact.

Did you know people seize you up and form an opinion about you in the initial 4 seconds of your first interaction with them? Make each second count. A firm handshake conveys confidence, affability and positivity. It symbolizes the unison of two powers that can come together to create something formidable. Powerful leaders always shake hands in a manner that conveys their strength and control.

Do not use random, distracting or nervous gestures while addressing your group. Use gestures that complement verbal communication. For instance, if you are talking about a job well done or appreciation directed your company's way, use the thumbs-up gesture. These gestures support your speech, and create a memorable impression in the minds of followers.

Always maintain a powerful posture. Strong leaders communicate confidence, self-assuredness and strength very subtly through their posture. Keep you posture outstretched and open to project transparency, confidence and power. Your head should be straight. Make unwavering eye contact while talking to people. Do not forget to smile.

One of the neatest tricks before an important presentation is to practice postures in front of a mirror. You will invariably feel more confident, and subconsciously convey to your audience that you are totally in control, positive about the organization's future and capable of setting powerful goals. When on stage, try to walk, pause and walk again for greater effect rather than making erratic movements or remaining stationary. Movement depicts energy, enthusiasm and engagement, which can be highly contagious for followers.

Anxious gestures such as pulling at your shirt collar or lifting your hair indicates a bundle of nervous energy, which does little to assure followers in a crisis. Employees expect leaders to be calm and in control of the situation when they are rattled. If they detect nervousness in your body language, they tend to lose confidence too. Keep your body language calm, cool and collected to re-establish security. This comforts followers, and facilitates collaboration.

Think Before You Speak

A young boy aged 15 years and his father occupied the seat of a train. There was a large group of friends sitting on the seats adjacent to them. The young boy was surprised and startled to see everything. He exclaimed, "Look the train is moving and things are going backwards." The father simply smiled and acknowledged. As the train picked up speed, so did the boy's excitement. "Look the trees are green and are running backward so fast." The dad smiled again and gave him an encouraging look.

The group of friends was watching the boy with amusement

and asked his father "Is your son suffering from a problem? Why is he behaving so weirdly?" One of the boys simply shouted, "I think he is mad." The boy's father replied in a calm and patient manner, "My son was blind since birth. He was operated upon a few days ago and got his vision. He is seeing these things for the first time in life." The group went quiet and immediately apologized to the father son duo for their blunder.

Like the group of boys, sometimes we just assume things and speak mindlessly. There is no conscious thought on speaking the right things or the effect our words will have on people. Focus on saying the right thing. Use words that motivate, inspire, assure and build people. Matters can be fixed if we say the right things at the right time, and can snowball into a disaster if we use the wrong words without thinking.

Be tolerant and listen to the other person's point of view. Do not just pretend to hear people but listen to them closely. Engage yourself, and show empathy without being judgmental. Do not listen to get a validation of your opinions or have your ego stoked.

Eliminate distractions while having conversations with your team, watch out for non verbal clues and control your reaction. You may be tempted to react in a particular manner impulsively. However, hold back until you completely hear them out. Do not jump to quick conclusions or judgments. If what they are saying is not clear, simply ask questions or paraphrase for clarity.

Chapter Three: Dealing With People

Remember the famous Maya Angelou quote, "I've learned that people will forget what you said, people will forget what you did, but people will never forget how you made them feel?" This is a million times true. People will never forget how you make them feel. The way you deal with people and treat them is a solid reflection of your own character. It is often said if you want to truly judge a person's character, observe the manner in which they treat people who can do nothing for them.

Be Genuinely Concerned

Show genuine concern for your staff, customers, volunteers, business associates, service providers, shareholders and all those who are closely associated with the business. Reach out to people in a way that makes them feel looked after and cared for. Place the welfare of people above everything.

Be genuinely concerned about the well being of everyone involved in the organization. When you treat people well, they respond with equal respect, a strong sense of loyalty and a feeling of belongingness, which is crucial for low attrition and overall job satisfaction. Watch what you say to people.

A leader is always comfortable sharing spotlight and credit for great results with his team. Humility originates from confidence, which is absent in leaders who are always eager to hog praise and recognition themselves. Your employees will be driven to achieve even greater results when they feel a part of the organization's success. They will appreciate how you make them feel and work with a higher sense of loyalty to earn your pride.

Abraham Lincoln genuinely cared about people and made an effort to demonstrate his humanitarian instincts at every given opportunity, which is why he is revered by generations. The leadership genius of Lincoln is that he intuitively understood that employee/follower performance is directly affected by emotions and feelings. He cared about people, used encouraging words and communicated through remarkably thoughtful gestures to assure people of their individual genius. He indentified with the struggles of people and garnered a huge influence due to his empathetic leadership style. In the words of Abraham Lincoln, one of the world's wisest leaders, "In order to win a man to your cause, you must first reach his heart, the great high road to reason."

Discard Grudges

As a leader, it is critical to set the rhythm for a more inclusive organizational culture that thrives on progress, positivity and forgiveness over back-biting, vengeance, and loose talk that can hinder productivity. Since leaders operate at the focal point of human relationships, every move of theirs should be directed towards setting an example for large heartedness and forgiveness.

Reflect and remind yourself that holding a grudge or ill feelings against people builds negativity in you. It soaks your energy and may lead to irrational or negative actions. It takes away the focus from productive goals. Walk in someone else's shoes. Imagine yourself in their place to try and understand what drove them to behave the way they did without harshly judging their actions. You do not have to endorse or whole heartedly agree with their actions. Try and see where they are coming from.

Rather than holding grudges and seeking vengeance, talk to the person honestly about how you felt and get it over with. You will feel better and less prone to housing grudges after expressing yourself. Forgiving and forgetting the act needs closure. Do not speak to people in anger, while also freeing yourself from holding any grudges against them. Also, if doesn't help to simply speak politely to people on the face and hold grudges against them within you. Get rid of all ill feelings internally and externally. Show compassion, speak gently, try and understand what led people to behave the way they did and forgive them inside out.

One of the best strategies for discarding grudges is to come to some sort of an understanding with a person or group of people. Get clear assurance that people will not repeat their actions. This will gradually help you re-establish trust and eliminate grudges.

Forgiveness doesn't make you any less of a leader. It doesn't imply that you are not operating from a power position or surrendering your dominant role. It simply means you are wise enough to let go negative emotions and focus on positivity for increasing the organization's productivity.

Be Positive

Be positive is the blood group of all leaders. On a more serious note, everyone has some positive and negative characteristics. If you've found the perfect being, you probably exist on another planet. Great leaders know the value of cultivating a culture that encourages employee errors as a way for learning and growing. Though this sounds overtly optimistic, it leads to fewer errors in the long haul. Every failure can include some learning.

Rather than focusing on your employees' weaknesses, try and highlight their strengths even when referring to their mistakes. This gives a powerful positive twist to the process of evaluating their action. Let us consider an example. An employee Ann lacks time management skills due to which she missed a couple of deadlines. However, she is great with research.

Start by telling her how wonderfully well researched the project is and how much more appreciation it was capable of bagging had it been turned in on time. This doesn't make your team members feel devalued or de-motivated. They will be more driven and determined to learn from their mistake in future. Simply highlighting the negatives makes the employee's morale hit rock bottom.

One solid tip for gaining people's undying loyalty and allegiance is to be good to them when they least expect it. People automatically assume harsh reactions from leaders when they make mistakes. However, if you treat them gently and compassionately by highlighting their positives, you are only boosting their morale for not repeating the mistake.

Criticize or admonish the mistake not the person. A mature leader does not resort to name calling and launching personal attacks. People get frustrated and demoralized when you criticize them rather than singling out their acts. It builds resentment and rebellion in followers. People will not be very comfortable openly discussing matters with a leader who resorts to criticizing them over their acts. When people make mistakes, they are already feeling miserable about it.

Speaking harshly is like rubbing salt on their existing wounds. Do not say something like "you are such a terrible worker." Instead try saying "what you did was not the best thing to do. Instead you could have done this." This way you are still pointing out the mistake without coming across as personally offensive. Also, when errors happen and problems arise due to them, get rid of the blame game. Be a part of the solution instead of making people feel terrible about their mistakes. A good leader moves over from the problem and uses a solution oriented approach. Focus on how to remedy the problematic situation.

Comfort Followers

Always be a source of comfort for followers. People should be able to feel secure and comforted in the bleakest hours. Do not be a source of depression, negativity, misery and disheartenment of your followers. How do you deal in situations where your spouse, employees, children and others close to you disappoint you? Do you react immediately and cause even more damage to the already volatile situation? That may not be the best way to deal with the situation.

It helps to comfort people when they make mistakes or disappoint you because this only makes them regret the mistake than get defensive about it. If you launch on an offensive, be ready to accept a truckload of excuses and defenses. Rather than blaming people or accusing them, try to win their confidence by talking sense to them.

Let us consider an example. An otherwise brilliant employee Rick has been rather disappointing in his latest project. Instead of belittling him for slacking, try and comfort him to understand what really led to this unlikely situation. Ask Rick if there is something you can do to help him. Try and find out if anything has changed over the past few days or if his morale is low.

Accusing and reprimanding people may not take you too far. You may not reach the root of the problem. Fear doesn't foster constructive talks. Let us assume Rick has made a new bunch of friends, who drink in the local bar until late night everyday, which has led to him not being able to give sufficient time to work. He may not share it with you if he finds your approach condescending and critical. Once you identify the problem, you can work together to resolve it. However, to pin down the problem, you need to be an approachable, assuring and comforting leader.

Value Your Team/Staff/Followers

Much as you believe you are the leader and an important person in the organization, try to imagine the state of your company's affairs if the staff does not turn up for work. Can your company function with their hard work and expertise? Do you value them enough? Do you let them know you value them?

Followers are always looking up to leaders, and are bound to feel a strong sense of emotional attachment with the leader. If as a business owner you only tend to focus on the top staff, the others are bound to feel unimportant or demoralized. They will be left with no option but to think, even though we exist here, only a handful of people's contributions are valued. They feel others are more important than them which invariably incites resentment.

These feelings directly affect employee morale, which in turn lowers productivity. It reduces work quality and employee satisfaction. If this feeling is harbored for long, you can be sure its pack up time for the business. People are your most valuable resource. If you cannot keep you internal customers or employees feel valued and happy, how do you expect to satisfy external customers? Profitable businesses understand the real value of keeping their employees happy.

Some of the best ways to make your employees feel valued is by letting them reward each other, spending more time with your employees, offering them a platform to share their expertise, making them a part of decision making, giving them small surprises, being specific with praise, publically recognizing their achievements, being transparent, giving them time off, encouraging their growth and organizing off-site events.

Treat Everyone With Respect

Imagine you are out on your first date with a person who appears to be everything you have ever dreamed of. They are charming, intelligent, humorous and adventurous, until you hear them show disrespect to a hapless waiter who is just doing his job. They turn back to you and again act their usual charming self. Are you convinced about him/her being a good human being or leader? Not really.

Leaders treat everyone with respect. In any relationship, if you do not treat people well, you are paving the way for them to run in another direction. Your employees are no exception. When you do not treat your employees well, they will quickly find opportunities where they are more valued and respected. Your organization will never be the same without them.

What happens when you drop a glass on the floor? It shatters and disperses into different directions. If you break the morale of your employees by ill treating or disrespecting them, they will disperse in different directions. You cannot put a broken glass together ever again. Even if you do manage to pull it off, the glass can never be what it was originally. Similarly, once your workforce disperses into different directions, it is near impossible to bring them back. Even if you bring them back, the pieces or employees will never fit in the same way again.

Always remember the good things people have done for your organization. Show them respect and appreciation for contributing to the overall growth of the business. Keep reminding them of the good they have done for the company, which will make them continue with it. People always reciprocate positively when they are awarded the respect they deserve.

Invest In Your Staff

Having empowered, excited and engaged employees can often be the difference between successful businesses and those struggling to find a foothold. Empowered employees who show initiative and complete tasks with little supervision can help a company fulfill its goals effectively. Focus on empowering employees by investing in them.

Encourage people by helping them move up the corporate hierarchy. If someone performs exceptionally well consistently, guide them to better opportunities within the company or outside it if required. Giving employees a clear career advancement path makes them work harder to achieve it. They will pitch in more in terms of insights and efforts if they are encouraged to go beyond their traditional roles.

Eliminate any potential hurdles that come in the way of employee empowerment in terms of organizational policies and practices. Facilitate a culture based on greater sharing and open communication. Encouraging employees to come up with new ideas, strategies and concepts is one of the best ways to empower them. Chuck the top down communication flow and invite employees to contribute their 2 cents for the overall development of your organization.

Give employees the tools required to lead, grow and succeed. Offer them specialized training, experienced mentors, specific feedback and everything else they need to be empowered. Several leaders complain how employees are stagnant but do not take a proactive approach in helping them grow. Employees are not always impressed with money or fancy designations. They are much likelier to stay in an organization where they feel a part of the company's success. An organization where they feel valued and empowered for developing their skills.

Chapter Four: Picking The Right People

One of the most vital ongoing responsibilities of a leader is to hire. It can be a highly challenging, time-consuming and crucial decision, which has the power to make or break your organization's reputation. Successful companies have mastered the art of hiring top quality candidates by evaluating them in multiple skill and personality areas. There is an increasing effort in getting to know people really well before hiring them. So, how do leaders of successful companies consistently hire a high quality, skilled, goal driven and efficient workforce? Here are some powerful tips to help you become the ultimate quality hiring rockstar.

Hire High Quality Staff

According to a Wall Street report, if companies are not careful about writing their job positing well, high quality candidates can be deterred from applying. Several companies focus on writing detailed and elaborate descriptions with a long winded list of requirements. However, researchers in the United States and Canada found that this practice only alienates great candidates.

Plenty of companies make the mistake of focusing on knowledge and technical skills, while overlooking soft skills. Is a candidate fit for a particular role personality-wise? Skills can be easier to acquire than personality. Social intelligence or the ability to tackle social situations is integral to several modern day job profiles. Emotional quotient, social intelligence, leadership skills, crisis management etc are crucial job skills that should be considered while hiring.

Does your hire's personality fit the role? Other than domain knowledge, good leaders pick their hires based on personality traits that match the job profile. The same trait can be a perfect fit for one job and completely unsuitable for another. For example, empathy would be a vital personality trait for a nurse but not for a software programmer or accountant. Similarly, the culture of an organization also determines the kind of people who would fit well.

Scan through the social media profiles of potential candidates for a quick and informal background check. However, do not take this to sum up the entire personality of the employee. This is just a way to help you get to know the person behind the corporate persona. Let this not be the only means of factoring hiring decisions.

Hire Folks Who Are Serious About Their Jobs

If you keep recruiting folks who are talented but do not approach their job with the right attitude, you'll be forced to hire every couple of months. These are the energy drainers who will not perform and will not others to perform by damaging their morale. You can have all the technical and social skills in the world, however it should also be backed by the right attitude and work ethics.

People who give priority to their work and are serious about implementing their duties do not need constant monitoring and work with minimal interference. This saves you the time and energy to be on their back constantly. Hire people who safeguard their job and implement their duties with diligence.

People with the right attitude will not sleep on their job or constantly take time off or try to bend the system using immoral or unethical ways. The honest folks will value their work and look after their job seriously. You have to display exceptional integrity as a leader if you want your folks to follow suit. Jon Hunstman, a multibillionaire who launched a chemical company from nothing and expanded it into a whopping $12 billion business recalled stories from his business experience where he absolutely refused to comprise on his integrity and principles in his book, Winners Never Cheat. Hunstman attributes his success to his honest approach.

People committed to their career or responsibilities make for ideal candidates. Opt for these folks over frequent career and job switchers, who simply shuttle between jobs for a few extra bucks.

Focus on hiring positive, committed and encouraging people who will boost the morale of other workers. Bad workers are like rotten apples who if kept along with good apples (good workers) will turn them into rotten apples too. It doesn't take much time for good workers to quit the organization for better opportunities. As a leader, you must be able to retain your star performers.

Hire Knowledgeable Folks

Hiring intelligent, knowledgeable, creative and analytical people is one of the best ways to ensure an organization's success. Look for people who are knowledgeable in their domain and possess superior industry expertise. They will be able to navigate through technical challenges and create solutions. Some leaders do not want their expertise or creativity to be outshined. However, having employees or team members whose brilliance surpasses your own empowers the leader to focus more on policy formation and other important goals at the corporate level rather than day to day functioning of the organization.

Rather than viewing someone's competency as a threat to your own leadership, view it as an asset for the company. Do not be intimidated by people who are more knowledgeable and experienced than you, and have the right attitude to place the organization's goals above everything else. Ask relevant questions during the hiring process to determine an individual's knowledge, industry expertise, skills and capabilities. Also, pick people who are constantly willing to learn over "know it alls."

Opt for people who encourage the idea of introspection, development and personal growth for everyone. This fosters a feeling openness, humility, learning and curiosity. A great leader always encourages his team to learn and growth.

Fire Lazy People

While this may appear harsh at the onset, leaders should be proactive in dealing with the "rotten apple" employees. This bunch lowers overall energy, enthusiasm and morale of the team. Whenever you discover someone is not performing up to the mark due to sheer laziness or has a casual approach towards work, simply replace them with more capable and conscientious employees.

Sometimes the managers or those in authoritative positions are themselves lazy, which fosters a laidback feeling among team members too. Identify and sack these slack managers. Lazy managers are going to invest little time and effort in coaching team members. They will not closely involve themselves in the day to day workings of their team, and pretty much leave the team to sort things on their own. They may not conduct regular team meetings or have briefings with the team to catch up on their progress.

Lazy managers do not focus on setting expectations or making team members accountable for those goals. They are simply happy to dump their responsibilities on other ignorant folks. This breeds a culture of de-motivation throughout the organization. Therefore, display the courage to fire lazy employees after a couple of warnings.

Delegate

Delegating responsibility for leveraging time and efforts is one of the best ways for meeting business goals. Real leadership is about picking the right people to perform tasks according to their individual skills and capabilities. This strategy optimizes the utilization of human and time resources to ensure multiple tasks are performed simultaneously. How much can one leader supervise? The idea is to create many more leaders who can be delegated with the responsibility of managing individual teams.

Imagine monitoring the day to day functions of 60 workers in contrast to having five capable leaders report to you with daily updates of their teams. Allocate responsibilities according to talent and experience. Workers feel good when their skills are acknowledged, and they are handed additional responsibilities.

Many organizations or government departments reshuffle staff according to their personal preferences. It is more based on people they like or dislike than real capabilities. Personal biases do not work well when it comes to handpicking people for delegating responsibilities. Select people who have a proven track record of turning in high quality work, have the attitude for the role and are industry knowledge savvy.

Hold Your People In High Regard

Hold everyone working in your organization with the highest regard. It can be anyone from your manager to the support staff to cleaner. They are all contributing to your organization's goals.

Each of them is important for the smooth functioning of your business. These are the pillars of your organization, who work hard to ensure the comfort of others. Can you imagine a day without the janitor or office cleaner? Wouldn't it cause inconvenience to everyone? Yet, people feel they are the insignificant folks who do not have an important role in the functioning of an organization.

Holding people in high regard and respecting everyone equally, irrespective of the position they hold in your organization ensures people feel a sense of belongingness and pride in working for you.

Chapter Five: Characteristics To Develop as a Leader

Leaders aren't really born. They are created. They are regular folks who work hard on building extraordinary characteristics. The good news is that all these qualities can be acquired or learnt. They can become your second skin with practice, discipline and repetition. Here are some of the most important leadership traits that people must possess in order to inspire their followers, and lead from the front.

Have you watched the Disney's *Lion King*? If not, I suggest you do it immediately. If yes, watch it again. This time for the innumerable leadership lessons it holds. It brings to mind Simon Sinek's quote, "There are leaders and then there are those who lead."

For those who aren't familiar with the basic plot, Scar is the discontented brother of king Mufasa. In his sinister bid to become the king, Scar tries to kill Mufasa and his nephew (the heir) at once. During Scar's rule, everything is in shambles. There's barely any food, the fertile land turns barren and animals begin leaving the kingdom.

There are many vital lessons here when it comes to being a

leader and influencer. Leadership is not having a bunch of followers who take orders from you. It is about inspiring, influencing and positively directing your tribe by leading from the front. Leadership is about using power constructively to bring about change and positivity.

Let's just share an amazing leadership story with you to whet your appetite for more to come. I particularly love this one leadership tale that exemplifies how a leader/influencer leads through example.

This is an anecdote about a leader known all around world for his principles of truth and non-violence.

A mother came to seek Mahatma Gandhi's help in getting her young boy to stop his sugar addiction. She had tried everything in the book to get him to stop his habit of consuming excessive sugar and finally knocked on the door of The Mahatma. She embarked on a long, arduous and tiring journey in the scorching sun, only to be told by Gandhi to return after a few weeks.

The lady was shocked. She had negotiated a journey spanning several miles just to get Gandhi to ask her son to stop eating sugar only to be sent back. "I can't tell him not to sugar. But return in a few weeks and then I'll talk to your son." The mother had no choice but to return home tired and dejected.

They returned after a fortnight. Gandhi welcomed them and

made direct eye contact with the boy, while telling him, "Boy, you shouldn't eat sugar. It is bad for your health." The boy nodded and vowed not to eat sugar. The mother was now flabbergasted. She simply asked, "Why couldn't you tell him this a fortnight ago?"

Gandhi smiled gently and replied, "Two weeks ago I was eating plenty of sugar myself."

A leader/influencer/role model leads from the front through their example. It is easier to draw people's faith and get them to listen to you if you practice exactly what you preach.

Good leaders know what motivates people and how to inspire them. They are humble approachable and value team-work. Here are some commonly researched traits that leaders and influencers possess.

Leaders are Learners

Leadership isn't the be-all and end-all of learning. If anything, good leaders know/recognize the value of leveraging by learning from different resources. They are constantly reading, watching industry related videos, learning from their team members and basically doing everything to stay on top of their game.

They learn not to show-off their knowledge but to be able to guide their team more efficiently. There is a never-quenching thirst to stay to date with recent trends and industry-related news. They will never hesitate to ask questions or have conversations that help them acquire knowledge. Yes, good leaders are phenomenal learners, which help them become better teachers.

Simba's influence as a leader grew only when he demonstrated a willingness to learn from Mufasa, Rafiki (the wise old baboon) and Zazu, the bird. True leaders/ role models are perennially committed to the pursuit of learning, growth, exploration and discovery.

Leaders Care

"People really don't care how much you know unless they know how much you care." If you aren't a caring empathetic and compassionate leader, your other strengths matter little to people. You may be an exceptionally skilled and gifted individual. However, lack of compassion kills it for leaders.

Influencers and leaders will eventually have people turn on them if they are merely drunk with a zeal for power without possessing the right emotions towards their followers. In the Lion King too, the lions preferred to starve to death over serving Scar. They felt a deep sense of betrayal. Even the hyenas (who felt Scar was their ally) dumped him eventually. When his true colors were revealed, everyone turned against him.

You aren't a true leader if you show scant concern for people's or your organization's well being. Good leaders are always high on empathy for their followers, and this naturally makes them more likely to be heard and admired by their followers.

Leadership is Not Power or Authority Based

Leadership is not about being high on the syndrome of power and position. You can't by default get people to obey you, follow your orders and generally bow down to you because you are their leader. A leader inspires faith and admiration, rather than expecting people to follow his commands blindly. If people merely fear you without looking up to you, there's something amiss in the leadership style.

If you are simply giddy with power and lack sensitivity or decision making skills (keeping the interests of your followers and organization in mind), you're far from being a true leader/influencer.

When Scar takes raises to the position of the king of Pride Rock, he expects everyone to follow his commands and obey him without questioning. However his vanity, poor decision making and lack of positive influencing contribute to Scar's undoing. People rarely accept leaders who shoot orders or misuse their authoritative position. Followers accept leaders who inspire and win their trust.

It is as simple as, lousy leaders only accept power, where as good leaders accept the well-being of their people before power.

Good Leaders Motivate

There is a popular quote that comes to mind, "a true master isn't the one who creates thousands of followers but he who creates other masters." Good leaders are threatened by the prospect of losing their hold on power. They encourage other skilled, talented and able followers to become leaders by guiding and motivating them in the right direction.

Great influencers are seldom insecure about their position and often go out of the way to mentor their followers into being capable leaders. When you encourage others, they gain confidence and high self-respect. This is a reflection of your own confidence and high self-esteem. When you show respect for yourself and others, it is easy to earn the respect and admiration for those around you. What goes around truly comes around.

Even while criticizing or giving critical feedback good leaders motivate. They use a concept commonly known as "the feedback sandwich", which is nothing but cushioning the wee bit unflattering statement with a couple of positive statements in the beginning and end. For instance, instead of telling someone that they haven't been much focused off late, start with how much you value the professional relationship, and how the company misses xyz's (employee name) focus. You can end with, "you really matter to the company so I really want to know, what's holding you back?" This is bringing the "not to nice things" to people's notice while still offering them hearty, genuine praise to prevent deflating their spirit. Leaders know how to balance critical evaluations with both - positive and negative feedback.

Good Leaders Reflect Integrity

Good leaders encourage their followers to act with honestly and integrity, following their own example. Integrity is at the basis of a powerful leadership. When what you say and do is in congruence with each other, it becomes easier to get people to listen to you. Honest, upright and truthful leaders always inspire the loyalty and faith of their people.

When you act with honestly, your followers respond with equal measures of integrity. You can't pull up others for their dishonest ways if you yourself are acting underhandedly. Positional leaders merely fill in a post for a particular time until it's time to be replaced by another leader. Transformational leaders, like the Lion King, rise to the occasion and seek to bring about a positive change in the lives of their followers through their own actions.

Influencers use their influence positively. They are aware of the fact that with great power also brings along a greater sense of integrity, responsibility and accountability.

How do you want to be remembered as a leader? Someone who impacted people's lives positively through example? Or someone who turned his/her back on his/her true responsibilities as a leader? The choice is yours.

Leaders Have Vision

Scar had zero vision or goals for his followers. All he wanted was power. This was rather evident towards the end, when food vanished from Pride Rock, and he was unwilling to make changes for helping his followers. The focus was entirely on his position as the king of the land. Such leaders have zero vision, and often point fingers at others or make others scapegoats for their mistakes.

This kind of leadership only harbours frustration and stress. A true influencer will have a strong vision about where his people or organization is headed. He will have clear goals, positive motives and well-planned action in place to meet his team's objectives. Effective leaders and influencers are willing to accept the responsibility for their actions when they backfire. They don't harbor selfish or vested goals at the cost of their followers' well-being.

Good leaders are aware of the duties and responsibilities that their position entails in the first place. They are aware of what is needed for them to do justice to the position they earned.

Being a role model is all about leading from the front, armed by a clear vision.

Good Leaders are Positive and Creative

Rather than being disgruntled about things that can't be done, resourceful role models resort to creating opportunities and resolving problems creatively. They are always upbeat, energetic and positive, offering everything from sound relationship advice to tips for enhancing work productivity. They exude infectious enthusiasm that inspires everyone in a positive direction.

Role models and influencers know to maintain a fine balance between productivity and fun. They keep the atmosphere around them positive. It is easier to earn the loyalty and devotion of team members (which in turn results in amazing results) if they work in good spirits. If your team works in an environment balanced with playfulness and efficiency, they are less likely to grumble about staying behind a few extra hours to complete an important report.

Good leaders and role models inspire devotion to the organization/brand. People are inspired to go beyond their call of duty if they feel good about themselves and the environment they work in.

Leaders Are Trustworthy and Transparent

Trust and transparency should be non-negotiable for leaders. Whatever ethical principles you otherwise hold on to, the responsibility of a team makes you accountable for acting with honesty and integrity. Your organization, employees and customers are a reflection of your own attitude. Raise the honesty bar higher if you want your team to follow you. Integrity is all about truthfulness. It is about being open, and telling the truth, however bitter, in all situations.

When you promote a culture of truth and transparency in the workplace, your team is encouraged to live up to those standards. You are influencing the entire organizational atmosphere to function with a sense of genuineness, which can be beneficial for everyone is the long run.

Integrity originates from a fusion of thoughts, feelings and actions. It is when we act from the core of our values. Mahatma Gandhi was one of the best examples of integrity. One of the many stories demonstrating his penchant for being a role model and leading by example will illustrate the lesson beautifully.

A young mother once brought her child to Gandhi, requesting him to ask the boy not to consume sugar because it wasn't good for his diet or growing teeth. Gandhi replied in a straightforward manner that he couldn't tell the boy that.

However he asked the mother to bring the boy back in a month. The mother was sorely disappointed. She had travelled quite a distance to meet the great man only to be turned back and called after a month. Yet, left with no option, she returned with her child.

A month later, she came back to Gandhi and repeated her request. This time, he knelt and held the child's hands and told him, "Please do not sugar little child. It isn't good for your health." The mother was thankful yet flummoxed. She curiously enquired, "Why couldn't you say this a month ago?"Gandhi replied, "a month ago, I was eating sugar."

Leaders Possess Abundant Optimism

Leaders realize the importance of optimism when it comes to boosting their team's morale and keeping the workforce perpetually motivated. Effective leaders understand that they will not be able to create happy and inspired teams unless they exhibit optimism.

Practice displaying a positive attitude even when things go awry. Create a relaxed and calm environment when dealing with a crisis situation. Things will go wrong as it happens in all businesses. However, how you react to these situations will determine how affected your team is by it. If team members work in a positive and happy atmosphere, they are more likely to pitch in when it comes to working overtime or harder for completing a task.

Much like optimism, negativity too is contagious. Leaders who are forever complaining and negative about circumstances beyond their control often trigger similar attitude in team members. Smile. Have a cheerful disposition. Compliment people. Keep your body language cheerful. Notice the huge difference this small change in your attitude brings to the overall atmosphere of your workplace.

Optimistic leaders always focus on opportunities through their highly magnetic attitude. Positivity enables greater open mindedness, collaboration, innovativeness and problem solving. It diverts focus away from the problem to the solution. It displays a more proactive than reactive approach to problems. Optimists are solution inventors who always seek to make a difference.

Leaders Desire to Serve

Leadership is not about attaining and enjoying a cushy power position where you can order others around. It comes with a strong desire to be of service to people. It has little to do with power and more with the desire to serve followers responsibly. It is about being a part of a process that seeks to improve lives of people over chasing titles or fancy positions.

Prior to Eleanor Roosevelt, the responsibility of the First Lady of the United States was restricted to playing hostess at formal political and diplomatic gatherings. Roosevelt's penchant for service transformed America's expectations from the office of The First Lady. She worked relentlessly for human rights in the nation and several other countries across the world to become an important part of the creation of the United Nation's Declaration of Human Rights. Roosevelt could have simply enjoyed her powerful title and position. However, she chose to utilize the power to bring about change and serve people.

Leaders Rarely Display Arrogance

Arrogant leaders often falsely believe that they are acting from a point of confidence. They fancy themselves to be self-assured go-getters. However, there is a fine line between arrogance and confidence. Arrogance works like a leader repellent. Confident leaders believe in capability to change the world. Confidence gives you the ability to motivate others, take risks and push your employees for achieving higher goals.

Arrogant leaders, on the other hand believe, they know better than anyone else around. They have a plus sized ego, and are unwilling to learn, develop or change. They operate with a belief that they are forever right and others are fools.

Arrogance destroys a leader's relationship with his team members. They do little to motivate their employees. Do not be an arrogant leader who is constantly engaging in one upmanship and self ego massaging. Rather than telling everyone about the wonderful things you've accomplished, encourage and teach your team members to achieve those results.

Arrogant leaders are not very open to listening, asking questions or attempting to hold meaningful conversations with their followers. The talk always centers on their accomplishments. They cut off conversation mid-way when they do not agree with people, and seldom display listening skills. A typical characteristic - they will continue looking at their phone, eating, replying to mails and other stuff when people are talking to them. Their behavior clearly indicates they give far more importance to other things than their employees.

These folks do not inspire hope and positivity in people. They are quick to shift the blame of failure on someone else's shoulders. They hardly accept responsibility or accountability when things go wrong but are the first to hog credit for achievements. There is no word called apology is their dictionary. This is a definite relationship spoiler. People will seldom trust you or feel inspired by you.

Let us consider the example of Adolf Hitler. As a politician, he displayed a rather capable demeanor. He put together a political party, wrote an agenda, identified key issues that echoed with the masses, outwitted his opponents and attained supremacy through dictatorship in a fairly constitutional manner. However, his arrogance made him an absolute war leader disaster. He did not have the foresight of determining that invading Poland could lead to war with Western Allies. This was followed by scraping the Versailles treaty and Austrian annexation.

Hitler lived with the belief that he was a truly infallible army mastermind who knew way better than his generals. When things failed, he insisted it was the incompetency of his generals and perpetually blamed them for letting him down. In his eyes, he could do no wrong. We all know where this attitude led him, don't we?

Leaders Possess Humility

Humility is an essential characteristic of a good leader, especially servant leaders. When you keep aside your ego, you get more realistic about problems. There is a greater focus on listening, admitting you are not aware of all answers and exhibiting your need to constantly learn from others. Your ego does not block your desire to gather information needed for accomplishing best results. Humility doesn't prevent you from sharing credit where it is due. It allows you to accept responsibility for your mistakes when you mess up.

Humility should not be confused with thinking you are weak or not confident about yourself. It simply means you possess the confidence and awareness to identify the goodness in others without feeling insecure. It means you are comfortable admitting you may have gone wrong, and that you may not possess thorough knowledge about your industry. You are happy to give credit where it is due.

Keep a humble approach and appreciate your workers. Plenty of managers today display acute arrogance and speak discourteously with their workers. These workers will sooner or later move to a place where they are treated with greater respect. Mangers tend to act unfriendly or unapproachable when it comes to dealing with workers. A good leader doesn't believing in scaring or intimidating people. He/she believes in being down to earth and treating everyone with respect.

Leaders with humility are gentle, readily accept their mistakes, forgive easily, display gratitude, recognize their limitations, are unafraid to share authority and constantly invite feedback.

Leaders Are Not Unnecessarily Dominating

This is especially true after a catastrophe. People will admire you when you have every reason to be angry but choose to be calm instead. Be soft when dealing with people who've been through a crisis situation, even if their mistake. If you are forever getting angry and reprimanding people, you will lose their loyalty. They will feel de-motivated, and eventually quit the organization.

It really doesn't help to throw your weight around and act like a boss even though you are the boss. Act like a team member. Your behavior should demonstrate you are one of them if you want people to feel comfortable working with you. No where should your actions make your followers feel you are way above them in stature. More than power, treat your role as one of guidance and service.

Rather than passing around orders arrogantly, see how you can make work easier for your people. Focus on helping, guiding, assisting and serving them. This will directly reflect in their productivity.

Leaders Have Patience

Great leaders are patient with their people. They realize no one is perfect and do not have unrealistic expectations from followers/employees. Patient leaders are mature enough to accept that people make mistakes. They recognize that training and developing people takes time and effort. These leaders encourage people to take on greater responsibility and learn valuable lessons from their errors.

Leaders should take their time to think through a situation when they feel agitated, frustrated or stressed. Take a few deep breaths each time you are tempted to let out the steam. Visualize how your behavior with affect the overall organizational goals.

Always think before acting and contemplate the results of your actions thoughtfully. Avoid making rash decisions or saying things in the heat of the moment. Learn to genuinely listen to people and raise positive questions rather than getting angry and humiliating them. Give people time to enhance their skills and work on their weaknesses.

In a frenzied, forever moving business culture, you are always looking for people who are quick, skilled and nimble. You want workers who get things done quickly and efficiently. You feel the need to act fast to prevent competitors from moving ahead. However, pushing people around unrealistically only makes them more rebellious. Have a policy in place where new hires are given sufficient growth and development time, before entrusting them with important tasks.

Chapter Six: Building a Vision For Your Team or Followers

A vision is a specific, distinct and well defined view of the organization's future. It is closely related to strategic progresses planned for the business. Great leaders always have a clearly defined vision that is communicated to employees in a way that facilitates commitment, loyalty and enthusiasm for the organization. Visions are used to inspire your workers and give them clear objectives to achieve. Leaders are experts in expressing a vision or using it to create a sense of oneness or inspiration among workers.

Creating A Vision

One of the most fundamental things that differentiate leaders from followers is their ability to make decisions and strategize, which reflects their perspective of what a business can be over what it is currently. A powerful leader creates trust by acting consistently in ways that are compatible with transforming the vision into reality.

Creating a solid vision is like motivating people to pitch in for a common cause, which can be a huge binding factor. A powerful shared vision fosters a feeling of oneness within people, and bonds them into achieving a common goal. Sharing a similar cluster of skills, values and commitment makes people feel an integral component of the organization, which can foster an increased sense of loyalty. Concerted actions and commitment of several members of an organization increases the possibility of accomplishing it.

Leaders always know the direction in which they are headed. They are focused on fulfilling clear goals, and have a plan in place for doing it. They are also able to inspire their followers for staying on track, and willing to put them back on track if they falter.

Setting Proper Goals

Have you thought where your organization/business will be about five years down the line? Are you absolutely clear about the primary objective of your organization at the present moment? Do you know what is to be achieved today?

There are a few helpful rules that make your task of goal setting easier. To begin with, set goals that motivate you. Ensure they light a fire in your belly and are relevant to you. The goals won't survive if you are not passionate about the outcome. They should be closely related to larger picture of your organization.

Set goals that are weaved within the high priorities of your life. If you lack this focus, you may end up creating way too many goals, making it virtually impossible to fulfill each one of them. Make sure the goals are important for you and your followers, and there is some real value attached to fulfilling them.

Set goals that are precise and can be measured, so people know where exactly they are placed in the goal achievement process. You can't simply say your organization's goal is to decrease expenses. Do you want to reduce 1 percent expenses in the next couple of years or a 5 percent in the next 5 years? Be precise with goals so they are easier to achieve and measure. A well defined and measureable goal gives your followers something to work with. With measureable goals, you may not be able to celebrate the milestones of achieving them. These little celebrations can go a long way in boosting your team's morale.

Also, be realistic when it comes to setting your goals. Setting goals that are virtually impossible to attain can sag your team's morale. It can make them feel unproductive and demoralized. Unrealistic goals can be major confidence killers. On the flipside, setting goals that are too easy to achieve can create complacency within the organization. It can also foster a feeling of non-achievement. The ideal is to set balanced goals, which are realistic yet award people with a strong sense of accomplishment.

Keep Hope Alive

With constant changes in the workplace, a fluctuating economy and several other factors, employees are perpetually paralyzed by insecurity. As a leader, you should be able to make a positive impact in the lives of your employees/followers. They are always looking for motivation, hope and inspiration.

Former U.S.A. President Barrack Obama proved how hope can be a cornerstone of a successful leadership. Hope was a major component of both his Presidential campaigns in 2008 and 2012. American voters wanted a ray hope to latch on to. They wanted to strongly believe that there was a solution to their problems. They wanted to feel better about enjoying a brighter future. Obama's messages of *Hope and Change* (2008) and *Forward (2012)* hit the hammer on the nail.

Obama achieved results that many thought were virtually impossible from a Presidential candidate in the midst of one of the most challenging economic situations in recent times. He successfully sold hope to people who were insecure about their future.

When followers feel uncertain or troubled in their work or life, all they need is hope. As a leader, if you are unable to feel hopeful for a brighter future of the organization, there are slim chances of inspiring others to feel the same. Dejected leaders do not create hopeful followers. During the bleakest times, people want leaders to assure them that things will be fine soon. They are looking for some security that their fears and worries are unfounded.

Strategic Planning

Leaders should possess exceptional strategic planning skills. The objective of strategic planning is to set business objectives and develop a solid plan to achieve it. It involves taking a break from daily affairs, and focusing on the direction in which the business is heading and what its priorities should be.

Leaders should spent time identifying exactly where they want to take the organization and how to get there. They should be able to build all the risks and contingencies into the plan. They should also be able to guide followers/employees into navigating those risks and taking charge of the process of moving ahead.

As the business gets larger and more complicated, policy formation will require more sophistication. Leaders should be able to collect and analyze information to make beneficial decisions. You may need to look at how businesses operate and how conditions are developing in existing and prospective markets.

Strategic planning is a litmus test for any leader as it requires specialized planning and decision making skills. Think of a strategic plan as a road map for a successful business journey. As a leader, you need to anticipate what is coming up next and lead your team by suggesting the most effective routes to reach their or the organization's goals.

Focus

When leaders hit crunch, their ability to keep their followers focused is the clincher between success and failure. You may not be able to complete everything if you take on multiple tasks or projects. Therefore, learn to prioritize and focus on one task at a time. One of the best ways to achieve this is by weighing everything on an urgent and as well as important scale.

So, basically as a leader you determine if a task is important, urgent, both or neither. Priority should be awarded to tasks that are both urgent and important. When it comes to picking between the two, you may have to give priority to the urgent task, while neither neither urgent nor important should be your last option.

As a leader, you should be able to train your team to prioritize tasks and focus on a task single-mindedly for achieving stellar results. As a thumb rule, keep in mind that each minute spent planning can save you about ten minutes in execution. Put together a daily, weekly and monthly to do list that makes it easier for you to focus on high priority tasks.

Chapter Seven: Consultation For Decision Making

Consultation is a vital component of several types of leaderships such as consultative and participative leader. Consultation increases the participation of people in the decision making process, which makes them feel more valued. Employees need to feel happy and wanted in an organization to perform. When a leader consults with those below the established hierarchical tree, barriers are broken, paradigms are challenged and productivity increases.

You Are the Decision Maker

Though a leader is responsible for wielding the final decision, he/she will be more successful if he/she creates new channels for facilitating horizontal and vertical communication within the organization. This adaptive, open and flexible culture paves the way for more innovative ideas. Build a work culture where each person is comfortable in contributing ideas and suggestions for achieving the organization's goals. Though you listen to all suggestions, keep in mind that the final decision is yours.

Consult Executives

Be open and consult with executives. Listen to their suggestions and ideas. Feel genuinely concerned for people you wish to lead and serve. Involve them in the decision making process. If there is something that is going to impact them directly, allow them to share their ideas about it. Try to make things easier for your people.

Do not be biased against employees who've messed up before. Everyone deserves to have their voice heard. Do not discard opinions simply because you don't like someone or they made a mistake earlier.

The focus should be to consult all your staff and not just those in managerial or executive positions. Also, do not make a pretense of taking their opinions to superficially show them you care. Be genuinely interested in taking their suggestions for improving things within the organization. People are smart, and can call your bluff when you simply make a farce of inviting their suggestions without awarding much importance to it.

A majority of the existing leaders simply hear but do not listen or feel what their subordinates are trying to communicate.

Consult With Regular Staff

Consult with regular staff for their opinion. All people have unique and interesting ideas, which should be heard. You never know which staff member can come up with a highly innovate suggestion or solution to revolutionize the way your organization works. It is simply about keeping your ears open for constructive and meaningful ideas. People feel differently, view things differently and have varied positions on things. This brings more variety to the process of consultation, and increases its effectiveness.

Avoid taking criticism personally and accept feedback well. It can be demoralizing to be told something hasn't been done well. However, true leaders will seize this as an opportunity to up their game rather than wallow in self pity. Take feedback, suggestion, advice and reviews as learning for improvement. How else will you be a better leader? Keep asking for feedback if you want to keep getting better.

Show understanding and tolerate people you do not like. Try and view things from their perspective. What directs them to behave the way they do?

Listen for opportunities to learn new things that might impact the organization's present and future. Be tolerant and respect various points of view without being prejudiced. Accept difference of opinions in a healthy, mature and constructive manner. Do not take it personally when people disagree with you.

The Consultation Process

Most managers and leaders like to believe that they involve their team in the decision making process. However, are you truly engaging your employees in making crucial decisions?

It can start with seeking ideas, strategies, options and suggestions from employees. As a leader, you can also solicit opinion on decisions that are bound to directly impact a department. This can be followed by the leader implementing the idea if it is found to be viable.

You can also allow the team or department heads to make decisions about their teams with implicit trust in their abilities. Be ready to forgive people if they make mistakes and encourage them to find independent solutions for their problems.

Chapter Eight: Develop the Confidence to Start Asking

We've been constantly fed on psychological theories on how just about anyone can become a leader. It is easy, right? A few leadership tricks up the sleeve and whoosh, you're an able leader. Nope. That's not the way it works in the real world. Genuine leaders are rare, simply because not everyone is willing to do the one huge thing they really need to for building their influence. Not everyone becomes a leader. But does everyone have it in them to become one? A resounding yes.

What is the one thing that the planet's best leaders know and the average folks don't? How do they connect with the world's movers and shakers, while spreading their wings? You'll notice that while some people are constantly growing from strength to strength (writing guests blogs, networking with the big players and growing their business), others are struggling to stay afloat. Even with all other things being the same. What is that one trait that separates winners from average mongers? Why do some people keep growing their influence over the years? This blatantly simple yet overlooked secret has been closely guarded by everyone from dynasties to politicians to salesmen to large corporations.

The answer is not really what you're prepared for – Ask. Stumped? Why do we overlook something so basic? You may not be a persuasive or charismatic leader (heck, most average folks aren't and if you are, hello John. F. Kennedy!) or even possess inherent communication skills for winning people. You may be struggling with confidence or self-esteem related issues. You may not have any special skills for wooing people (let's just assume there's nothing extraordinary about you).

However, you have that one special weapon, which though everyone else has, few use. This naturally gives you an edge over others who do not use it. The power to ask. Sometimes, you'll be surprised at what you'll receive when you simply ask. By not asking, your chances of getting what you want are 0%. However, by asking, there is at least a small percentage, a teeny-weeny chance of you getting what you want.

How many times have you written to the Queen of England or the Dalai Lama or other international/ figures celebrities? None? Why? Owing to heavy doubt that these extremely busy figures will never make time to reply to an inconsequential individual like you. Yet, you'll be surprised to know how many living rooms across the world are adorned with letters from these seemingly elusive international figures. Why did some people get them while others didn't? Simply because the ones who got them increased their chances by asking.

Want a great worker to be a part of your team? Ask. Looking

for a promotion or raise? Ask. Want to make a business decision keeping the interests of your employees? Ask.

A small act of asking can trigger a large chain of events and open up bountiful opportunities for you. You never know when one opportunity leads to another, and ultimately takes you places, while increasing your influence. Leaders and influential folks are not a result of fluke. They know how to go out there and ask for exactly what they want or what they want others to do.

Sometimes even the biggest folks make themselves open and available to new ideas presented by seemingly "average Joes", so go out there and ask. You may want to create a social campaign or drive in your local area, and may need volunteers or the support of your community. How do you get it? Ask. Those bold enough to ask are often rewarded many times over simply because they dared to ask.

Asking is the difference between being a bestselling writer with copious royalty and a struggling writer whose manuscript is still collecting dust on shelves. When you ask, you boost your chances of making it happen, and create a series of favorable, fortunate conditions for yourself. As you can see for yourself – it isn't much about luck. It is about unlocking a treasure trove of good fortune and influence simply by asking. The new-age leadership is all about accessibility, and they are waiting to reach out to people who care to simply ask.

The number one trait that probably keeps us from succeeding or gaining influence is self doubt. We have this lousy habit of not considering ourselves worthy or deserving enough of greatness. The belief that we "don't have what it takes to succeed" or fear of failure/sabotage ruins more lives than actual failure.

Sometimes we just make up our mind in a single, constricted direction, and no amount of persuasion works. In simple words, we are our most lethal enemy. How many times have you stopped yourself from mailing a person who can grow your influence simply because you thought that the person will be too busy to respond?

A while ago, I persuaded a cousin to email someone she has greatly admired over the years. She just wouldn't send that email because her mind was already made up. She had automatically assumed that this person was way too occupied to respond to an insignificant nobody like herself. I tried every trick in the book to convince her, and ultimately got her to send the email. Bingo, the person responded almost immediately.

My cousin just couldn't believe what had happened. In her mind, she had already said "no" and shut herself from the prospect of getting a reply. Want to know a secret? Most people are accessible if we just believe that we are important enough for them to be glad to hear from us.

Want to connect with someone? Invite someone for coffee or dinner? Go on a date? Get someone's contact details? Get a meeting or appointment? Ask. The ultimate secret to winning a large following and influencing people is that just about anyone can achieve it. All you have to do is – ask.

Sometimes you have everything going for you in terms of skills, abilities and more, and yet you wonder why you aren't successful when it comes to influencing people or networking with powerful folks to grow your influence. Simple – you hesitated to ask. In your mind, you've already negated the prospect.

There's an easier way to get what you want or as they the old saying goes that the quickest route between two points is often a straight line. Though we come up with multiple convoluted plans and complicated strategies, the simplest way to get people to do what we want is to ask them.

Why are you wallowing in self-pity while your crush has gone out on a date with someone else? You feared rejected or coming across as stupid. And now the joke is on you, harsh as that sounds. Asking someone out or for what matter anything can be a scary prospect. However, isn't it better than simply waiting? Or letting a brilliant opportunity slip from right under your nose.

There's something irresistible about confident, self-assured and controlled folks that get them the desired attention. You bring the spotlight on you when you set aside all shreds of nervousness and ask. Be normal. Relax. Leave aside all nervousness. Be assertive yet polite while asking. More often than not, you'll get exactly what you want.

However, please don't consider asking as the magic diamond bullet for success. Sometimes, you'll got to be prepared to get no for an answer, which is alright since not asking is a downright no anyway. You may ask for leave, and not get it. You may ask for volunteers for a community drive and not get them. People may spend some time in consideration and refuse. That still pretty much comes close to not asking at all. At least, you'll have the satisfaction of trying. And you never know, you may be paving the way for future opportunities.

One of my actor friends auditioned for a role much against her wishes (she knew she wouldn't bag it and it would kill her spirit). As predicted by her, she didn't manage to snag the much coveted role. However, the auditioners kept her details on file, and contacted her for another role (pivotal to the plot) a few months down the line. She bagged the role, performed wonderfully, and even went on to bag a few more productions post to launch a successful stint. If opportunity doesn't knock on your door, build more doors and move.

People who know exactly what they want are greater leaders and influencers. When you ask for something, make sure the request is specific. This makes it easier for the other person to establish intentions and give you exactly what you want. Your request comes across as limp when you are unsure about what you desire. Part of being a good asker is to be specific about what you want and show the other person about how badly you want it.

Another asking tip that may appear counterintuitive to the above tip is to be flexible when you ask. For instance, if you want a long leave, you've got to be prepared to resume at a different position, with a different set of responsibilities. People who are too rigid with their demands don't go a long way. You have to be prepared to accept or compromise on certain aspects to gain something else.

People genuinely want to help each other in general, so it's unusual for someone to run down a valid, thoughtful and polite request. Most people feel good when they make a difference in someone else's life. They were probably in your position a few years ago, and relate to your request. Keep this in mind, and you'll feel confident enough to take on the world. And this will be your first step towards bagging that coveted "yes".

Also, you may have quickly resorted to influencing people without trying to win them over or strike a friendship with them. People don't take too kindly to being used, you know. Try to forge connections and friendships with people by asking, before jumping in with your motives. Learn to listen more and talk less about yourself. It isn't always about you.

You may be a fabulous performer but in all probability the lead role may have gone to the confident performer who dared to ask for it. Don't sabotage your own dreams and aspirations by not asking. Act now. Start asking. The difference between leaders and followers is leaders dare to ask and chase their goals.

Chapter Nine: Solid Tips For Increasing Your Influence Over People

In his international bestseller *The 7 Habits of Highly Effective People,* author and motivational speaker Stephen R. Covey elaborated how truly effective folks, who are constantly engaged in expanding their influence, lead a life focused on brining about a positive change within their circle of influence (areas that are within their control). They overlook things they have little power over (circle of concern) in favour of things they can proactively change. They divert their positive, magnifying and generously enlarging energy to increase their circle of influence. Here are some foolproof steps to increase your influence.

1. Practice Empathy

People who are able to recognize, feel and understand others' emotions can relate to their followers or others brilliantly. This makes them comes across as more compassionate and sensitive beings that are completely clued in to the feelings of others. It is fairly easy to influence and lead people when you win their faith by relating to their feelings. However, keep in mind that there is a difference between using empathy to influence people and manipulate them. Stay miles away from manipulating emption people trust you with.

2. Be Proactive

Influence cannot be grown by lying still. It happens only when you engage in the right activities, develop the right habits and surround yourself with the right people. Being proactive means going out there and forging new connections by constantly meeting new folks.

Proactive people don't wait for opportunity to knock on their door, they go out there and create multiple doors for themselves. They take courses, read books, sign up for newsletters/updates, and listen to podcasts/audio book. These are the real influencers and role models.

3. Accept Responsibility For Your Decisions

One of the most significant qualities of an influencer/role model is his/her ability to accept responsibility when things go awry and give credit wherever due. This trait alone makes a person/leader highly endearing to his followers. There's plenty of respect to be won when you are honest enough to admit you goofed up and accept responsibility for your actions rather trying to pass the buck on to someone else.

When you accept responsibility for your own and your team's actions, you quickly grow your influence by building others' trust in you.

3. Show Abundant Passion And Enthusiasm

Have the proverbial fire in your belly for whatever you do. This makes you an irresistible influencer. People can tell the difference when leaders/role models do something just for the heck of it and when they are truly operating with endless reserves of passion. Seeing you demonstrate the right amount of passion and commitment towards a project/cause lights others up too. This in turn grows your influence. It attracts others to work with you in your undying quest.

4. Stay Consistent

Consistency and commitment is a huge influence catalyst. It accelerates your influence in the positive direction by revealing how dependable your actions. People who are reliable, steadfast and dependable earn greater respect and obedience that people who constantly change their actions based on what suits them.

Keep your actions and words consistent. Stay consistent with the rules you make. Be consistent in your attitude, policies and leadership pattern. Above everything, stay consistent with your efforts for fulfilling your/the team's goals. People who don't give up are able to attract plenty of followers. Consistent folks are seen as reliable and are the preferred ones to be trusted with brand new projects, initiatives and responsibilities.

5. Find Solutions

Solution providers are always more sought after than problem diggers. Your influencer invariably increases if you possess a solution oriented mindset. People flock to leaders/role models who have a more solution focused mindset, and are capable of coming up with ingenious solutions to the most convoluted problems.

Folks who use lateral thinking, constructively problem solving skills and path breaking solutions are often people magnets. They become instantly dependable and likeable for their innovative thinking and positive approach.

6. Ask Questions

It's puzzling how little people value this one single trait that can make the quickly endearing towards others. So many people choose to ramble only about themselves and overlook the need to know more about others. Display natural curiosity in people to come across as an interesting conversationalist.

People misleadingly believe that reciting a witty anecdote or intelligent incident makes they come across as a stimulating conversationalist. Wrong. It is showing interest and curiosity in the other person (not bordering on excessive curiosity if you get what I mean, don't start an FBIish interrogation) that endears you to other people and gets them to listen to what you have to say.

Talking about yourself is not just boring, but plain rude and repulsive. In whichever social or business situation you are, asking questions is a fool proof way to get people to like you and influence them. "So, how's work?" "What are your plans for summer?" "Which was the last film you watched?" Appear genuinely interested in other folks to pique their interest in you. Be an awesome listener, and you're on your way to being a social rockstar.

7. Point Out Mistakes Constructively

The surefire way to earning a large bank of haters is pointing people's mistakes to them in a manner that destroys their self-esteem. Point out people's errors in a positive, healthy and constructive manner if you really want them to like you or listen to you.

Stay humble, grounded and neutral in your correction technique. Your feedback will be more heard and valued when you do it in a more rational and less offensive manner. People are less likely to listen to you or act upon your suggestion if you take off on a never-ending and vengeful rant.

Make it clear to a person that you aren't targeting them but only helping them or saving them from further embarrassment. Try something along the lines of, "Hey Roger, I noticed a few errors in the way you created those formulas on Excel. It isn't a huge deal of course, but you can start working on the smaller ones and work your way up if that sounds good. You can watch me do it too."

This sounds more honorable and is more likely to be heard by the other person than, "you're an absolute dud with mathematical formulas on Excel", which only ends up targeting the individual personally and makes them more defensive rather than open to suggestions.

If it's a paper, performance or project you are reviewing, do it constructively by starting with all the great things about it. Gently point our areas where there is scope for further improvement without sounding harsh. "Hey Simone, you've done xyz exceptionally well. However, I think you should go over abc once again because I feel you can add some more bits there to make it more power-packed. This will make your paper even more awesome."

Stay miles away from criticizing people in a rude, patronizing, blunt, harsh and exasperated way. It is always advisable to keep away from correcting people in public. Keep it limited to the two of you, and the person will truly appreciate it, while taking constructive steps in the right direction.

At times, it helps to save people's face even when you know they are wrong. This inspires them to bring about a positive change and makes you comes across as more likeable.

For instance, if you made a huge mistake in your workplace,

instead of pointing you out publically, if your boss only makes a general mention (so as to ensure that it's not repeated) without naming you, won't you develop greater respect for him? What he would've named and shamed you publically even when you know you goofed up big time? You would've hated him for life. While both reactions serve similar goals, the former is more constructive in bringing about the required change.

The other side of this, leaders who are quick and emphatic when it comes to admitting to their mistake make themselves instantly endearing to their followers. When you don't admit to your fault and try to make someone else the scapegoat or pass the buck elsewhere, it creates feelings of animosity and increases the hate quotient directed towards you. On the other hand, you earn huge reserves of respect, loyalty and credibility when you own up to your fault. People admire honesty, which further inspires them to have faith in you.

8. Agree to Disagree

Opposing views do not mean you have to turn your home, office or social club into a battle field. People who agree to disagree politely earn much more respect and influence as opposed to people who shove their views down other's throats and completely shut off to any view apart from theirs.

It is natural for people to hold different views. Not everyone is raised in the same circumstances or background as you. People come with a whole lot of different experiences, circumstances and life struggles, which tints their opinion or views on different subjects. Seek to understand where they are coming from rather than being fixated with the notion of "they are wrong and I am right."

Figure out what motivates them, appreciate their different beliefs (even if it doesn't match yours), and put across your views in a factual and respectful manner without tearing them apart. People who respect others' opinions increase their chances of being heard and understood. Others are less likely to get defensive and more eager to give your views a fair hearing if you appreciate their opinion, and take a more neutral stand.

As Dale Carnegie famously stated, "The only way to win an argument is to avoid it." Arguments, however healthy you think they are, are roadblocks to communication. Arguments cause a breakdown in the communication pattern. It doesn't foster any genuine information flow, makes things increasingly awkward and creates an atmosphere replete with bad vibes. In the end, the topic doesn't even matter. Everyone forgets what the argument was about, and only remembers the acrimony it caused. So chuck it really or put across your view in a more compassionate manner.

You don't have to agree with everyone. However, showing a

little empathy and compassion for other's views goes a long way in ensuring a healthy and open-minded debate, which ultimately helps grow your influence.

9. Compliment People Generously

This isn't a secret. Yet it is astounding how many people actually fail miserably when it comes to simple acts such as complimenting people. Why is it so tough to offer compliment people sincerely? Do you know someone who is a great mother or writer or manager? Why haven't you told them yet?

At a deeper, subconscious level, we all yearn for appreciation. When you appreciate people openly and regularly, they'll develop an instant liking for you. However on the flip side, don't use this weapon to resort to flattery. People are smart and can quickly differentiate between sycophancy and fake flattery from genuine compliments.

To make the compliments sound sincere, pick specific aspects that you truly appreciate in the person. For instance, "the half man, half woman painting of yours totally nailed gender issues with a lot of sensitivity and depth of understanding" over "your paintings are truly amazing."

Giving specific, well-thought and heart-felt compliments is one of the best strategies for being the ultimate people magnet. Just keep it genuine. Dishonest flattery has the exact opposite consequence, and people are smart enough to know the difference.

10. Smile

Smiling is one of the fastest ways to get people to like you. With the amount of grumpy, scowling faces spotted on the street, little wonder that people who sport a smile become instantly likeable. It is the most universally understood gesture of warmth and affability.

Humans instinctively relate gestures such as a smile, touch, hug etc to affability. It makes us feel that the person smiling at us genuinely likes us and is interested in us, which makes us like the person, and return their smile to create highly positive vibes.

Research has consistently pointed to the fact that smiling helps elevate our own mood, since our mind feels the way our body acts and vice-versa. So the next time you want to go about influencing people or being a leader, who wields plenty of magnetism on his/her people, just smile generously. It will radiate your inner warmth, and make people take to you instantly.

11. Help Others Own the Idea

One of the most proven strategies for influencing others and getting them do to go your way is to help them think it is their idea, which will make them more acceptable and less critical about it. They will be more charged about accepting an idea that they own.

Use the reverse psychology technique by stating the opposite of what you intent to get them to do. For instance if you want to convince someone to go hiking with you, saying something to the effect of, "I really didn't think there was any use asking you to accompany me for a hiking trip since you're not an adventure-buff, are you? You're simply prying on what you think the person wouldn't do and feeding him/her with ideas.

Offer lots of hints, suggestions and clues to help the other person draw their own conclusion, which pretty much makes the ideas theirs.

This is a sum of how things go in our personal relationships as well, right? When you need something from your partner, you simply drop clues hoping they will pick it up and give you what you need to surprise you. How about leaving a bunch of travel brochures all over the place and then subtly stating you need a break from all of it? The idea will of course be someone else's. Wink wink!

12. Use a Person's Name or Appropriate Title

Dale Carnegie, author of the bestseller, *How to Win Friends and Influence People,* has explicitly stated the need to use someone's name to make yourself more likeable for the other person. According to the public speaking legend, an individual's name is the most pleasant sound they can experience in any language, and this has a direct bearing on how they view people who are constantly addressing the with their name.

Our names are an inherent part of our existence, and hence hearing them repeatedly sort of authenticates our existence. This in turn helps us develop exceptionally positive feelings about people who validate our presence. To influence people, you can address them as what you want them to be, so they subconsciously start thinking about themselves as just that.

For instance, if you want to get closer to an acquaintance or strike up a friendship with them, start addressing them as "mate" or "buddy" each time you speak to them. Leaders and influencers know how to get people to do what they want simply by addressing people correctly.

Address your employees, followers, customers by their name as much as you can. It establishes a more personal foundation for your communication/ connection. No one fancies being just another number or account. People appreciate the personal touch and human element involved in being addressed by their names, and invariably end up liking folks who constantly use their name.

Using a name, title or type of address can have power effects on the subconscious. The whole point is that if you pretend to be a particular person, you will end up being that person. It is a kind of self manifesting prophecy. Similarly, when you want to influence others, address them as what you want them to be, so they start subconsciously thinking of themselves as just what you want them to be.

Chapter Ten: Tips For Being a Leader Everyone Loves To Follow!

Your ability to communicate with others in a social set-up depends on several factors including culture, beliefs, personality, individual challenges and social skills. These factors collectively determine how charismatic you will appear to others while interacting with them. To improve your charisma, you have to develop a specific skill set that helps you communicate more effectively with people from multiple backgrounds. Here's a valuable 8-step plan that can put you on the highway to social popularity if practiced consistently.

1. Listen. Understand the fact that communication is as much about listening as it's about talking. The golden rule – 70% listening and a mere 30% talking. Listening to the other person gives you plenty of clues about his needs, life and views on various things. Listening to the other person intently makes him feel like you're interested in him and understand him. This process leads to better communication.

2. Gather as much information as you can. Sometimes when people come from different backgrounds/ cultures, their talks may not reverberate with you. Even within the same language, dialect or terminology may differ from place to place. It will

help to learn beforehand about the person's culture to enhance your ability to strike up a conversation with him. Important – if you don't understand a language a person is communicating in, tell him instantly rather than pretending to understand. Find a common language to communicate in, if possible.

It is alright ask questions if you don't understand. If a person is talking way too fast, using several unfamiliar phrases and leaving out crucial bits of information, if it alright to ask questions. For all you know, he might be talking to people who are used to speaking rapidly or might be aware of all the technical jargons he's using. Clarifying things not just resolves the confusion for you but also shows the person that you're actually listening to them with interest.

3. Talk clearly. Make sure to communicate clearly in a language that will be well understood. Keep your voice clear, well-intonated and in the right pitch avoid any miscommunication. The pace of your speech should be moderate enough to be comprehended by everyone. Don't talk too fast or slow. Articulate yourself well using the right words, tone, gestures and expressions.

Check if you're message is being understood. Keep your eyes open for non verbal clues displaying your message is actually being understood as intended. Signs like furrowed eyebrows could indicate some confusion. This can be your hint to slow down or switch to a more interesting topic. Check if you can continue with the same topic by asking a question.

4. Maintain effective body language. When you're communicating with people from different cultures and backgrounds, you'll have to rely a lot on non-verbal communication such as gestures, voice and body language. Keep your body language approachable and open. Don't stare at the floor or in another direction when talking to someone. Keep eye contact throughout the interaction. Don't appear bored, disinterested or keep checking your phone.

5. Recognize similarities. This is especially true when communicating with people from different cultures. Focus on similarities and build on them whenever you get an opportunity. It can be anything from your favorite cuisine to your favorite actor. This helps you create a nice common ground for building an effective connection. If you find yourself wearing similar shoes or clothes as the other person, don't forget to mention it. People don't open up very easily when they find themselves with people who are not very similar to them.

6. Celebrate differences. While you're focused on finding common ground, don't forget to appreciate differences. One of the key rules of talking to just about anyone involves a genuine appreciation of diverse cultures, values and beliefs. You may want to inquire about a song from another culture that the other person is particularly enjoying. The best way to show your interest and appreciation is to ask questions about the

artist, name of the song, musical genre and instrument. You can also ask about festivals and cultural celebrations to show the other person you're sincerely interested in learning more about the cultural differences.

7. Stay well groomed. Don't forget to shower before attending a social gathering. Maintain high levels of cleanliness and hygiene. Use a good quality deodorant, keep your ears and teeth clean, and put on a pleasant fragrance. You can also visit the salon, and get yourself groomed with a stylish hairdo, manicure/pedicure etc. Wear clean clothes that suit your body type and personality. Make a statement with your individual style. While all this may seem elementary, it's staggering how many people actually get it all wrong, and then wonder why people miles away from them!

8. A good sense of humor seldom fails to impress. You'd obviously have to judge when to and when not to use humor. If the discussion is focused on a serious topic like world hunger, you'd be really insensitive for making a joke out of it. However, there are several instances for you to reveal your lighter side with a few clever jokes and witty remarks. This is one of the best secrets to attracting a large crowd. People instantly take to someone who's laughing and sharing a comical situation. You will come across as a fun person who people will like to have in their midst.

9. Just be yourself. Be confident, free spirit and most

important – be what you are. There's no need to try and pretend to be something you aren't. Avoid being self-conscious and keep your confidence level high. When you feel good about yourself, the feeling invariably transmits to other people. Don't stress too much about what others think of you. When you too anxious, it shows and hinders your chances of enjoying pleasant social interactions.

10. Appear polite and amiable. Be genuinely interested if someone is talking to you. Throw in an occasional nod, use acknowledgments such as "I see", "great", "that's cool" and other encouraging phrases to show you're actually interested in and listening to the person. Be true and honest, and don't agree with or say things that you don't believe in. You're an individual with a right to your opinion, and some people may even appreciate a different stand. However, make sure you're always polite and good-natured in your interactions.

11. Laugh and the world laughs with you. An honest and full-throated laughter can be highly contagious. It not just reveals high confidence levels, but also shows how open and receptive you are to laugh without any inhibitions. It's a sign of possessing a sense of humor, and instantly draws people to you.

12. Stand up for your cause. If there's a particular issue you feel very strongly about, try and focus the conversation around it. When you are able to passionately talk about something close

to you heart or take a bold stand, you come across as highly inspiring to others. Ensure however that you stay away from highly controversial topics that can lead to acrimony, and put across your views in a non-aggressive and rational manner.

13. Enter confidently. One of the best ways to get yourself noticed, especially at social gatherings, is to make a confident and attention-grabbing entry. Don't look at the floor while entering the room, keep your head and back straight, avoid slouching, pull your shoulders slightly backward and let the hands remain in the sides. Don't stay for long at the entrance, and make a confident entry that immediately draws attention to your presence. A pro tip for grabbing more eyeballs is to have someone by your side while entering. It can be a friend or spouse or colleague. This is guaranteed to attracted more eyeballs.

Chapter Eleven: Tips For Being an Effective Leader at Business Networking Events

So, you're lucky or hardworking or both to get an entry into an enviable business event that features several people you've always admired and wanted to get in touch with. As a leader or representative of your team, you would do anything for that one chance to talk to them. How do you do that without looking like another starry-eyed fool or wannabe? How do you go about making a stellar impression on your business contacts as a leader and get them to notice you over dozens of other associates? Here's the key.

1. Use the location as a conversation starter. When you think you have nothing to talk about at a business networking event, focus the conversation on a specific location. It can be about the convention center or the city's downtown area or a destination itself. Ask location oriented questions if you're interacting with locals. They'll be flattered so you're so interested in their city/town. Anything geographic and location specific can be a safe and neutral subject for breaking the ice at a business event.

2. Seek advice. Seeking advice is a great way to make people feel important and get noticed at business conventions. It

serves a two way purpose. You get the valuable information you are seeking, and start off a conversation with someone more experienced. The advice may not be limited to business. You can ask them for movie recommendations or suggestions about good pubs, anything based on common interests. Everyone likes it when their opinion is actively sought.

3. Ditch the elevator pitch. There's this commonly accepted advice of always being ready with an elevator pitch for networking with people anytime, anywhere. It is like a carefully and cleverly drafted phrasing of what you do. However, rather than making it seem rehearsed and memorized, try to have a more engaging and personal conversation. People get tired of listening to impersonal, mechanical and stuck-record like talks. Incorporate some spontaneity in your talks, even if it is introducing what you do at business events.

4. Take small notes about the meeting. When you meet a business associate for the first time, use the empty space behind their business card to take down small notes about something vital or a few defining points of the meeting. This will give you more fodder for conversation when you spot them again. They will be impressed that you remember the details of your last interaction.

4. Keep a hand free for greeting people. Don't be so focused on having your hands full with food that you forget the entire purpose of the event. You should always have a hand empty to

shake hands with business associates who may come and greet you suddenly. This isn't a full course, sit-down dinner but a networking event.

5. Display your networking skills. This is a neat trick that works really well with practice. Imagine you're at a business event where you don't know many people. How do you give the impression that you're well networked and well-connected? It's simple really. Once you introduce yourself to people or get introduced to them, introduce the newest person you met to another person at the event. This way you're making everyone feel like you know a lot of people at the event and are well-connected.

6. Avoid selling and just listen. Don't just start selling to people you're interacting with for the first time. Use this as a valuable base to get to know them better, before pitching your products/services. Listen. Establish a trustworthy and credible relationship. The focus shouldn't be on selling but helping them buy by building a genuine association.

7. Ask intelligent questions. Whenever people share something with you, ask them intelligent questions about it to show that you've been paying keen attention to what they were speaking. People like it when others care and pay close attention to what they've been saying. It's like a good ego booster.

8. It is a great opportunity to start a conversation with

someone who is all by themselves. They will not only be able to give you undivided attention and focus, but will also be more open about sharing valuable information. When you see someone standing all by themselves in a corner, don't hesitate to approach them and initiate a meaningful conversation.

9. Use a person's name when you've just been introduced to them. For some reason people always shy away from using a person's name when they've just been introduced to them. They feel like it's to be done only when you know a person very well. Contrary to that, people will instantly take to you when you use their name about 2-3 times in the conversation after being introduced to them. This is also a clever way to practice remembering their name.

10. Avoid joining a group of 4 (or greater than 4 people) already engaged in a discussion. You can stand on the side but don't barge in until you've made sufficient eye contact and introduced yourself to everyone.

11. Avoid giving out your business card mechanically. Personalize the process a bit by writing your contact number. This will make the person receiving the card feel they've received something more personal, important and privileged.

12. Keep testimonials ready. Always keep the buzz about your products/services ready to showcasing previous achievements. It can be anything from social media conversation to Instagram

images to client testimonials. Create hashtags while posting information about your products/services in the social media for organizing the information and making it more accessible.

13. Dress well. Don't expect people to take you seriously if you don't look the part. This should be a no-brainer. But people still don't get it sometimes. To make a professional impression on people, you have to dress and look professional. Don't expect people to have a high opinion of you if you show up in an extremely casual, unkempt or disorganized manner. Choose something that makes you look and feel good. Flaunt a new pair of shoes, a brand new handbag or a wonderful dress – anything that makes you radiate confidence.

14. Listen before speaking. Here's a pro networking insider secret. Always let others talk first. Most people fail to realize that those who speak first are not given complete attention. This is because everyone else is preoccupied with thoughts of what they're going to speak next. If you speak first, the other person is only going to partially listen to you. Once you let the finish, they will listen to you with rapt attention in a more relaxed manner.

15. Don't go with friends. Sometimes people are so jittery about the prospect of attending a networking event that they prefer to tag along their gang of friends. Avoid going to business networking events with friends, even if they belong to the same industry. You will end up spending time sticking to people you

are already familiar with, and not grab the opportunity for reaching out to new folks as a leader and influencer. Your aim should be to reach as many people as possible, while building and developing new contacts. This gives you the opportunity to grow your influence as a leader, catalyst, negotiator or change maker.

16. Curate connections. Rather than trying to network with every person in sight, learn to categorize and build quality connections. Curate your connections well. Don't go on collecting every business card. Otherwise, you're not going to be any better than a cold calling salesman. Invest your time in a few quality connections rather than spending a little amount of time with everyone.

17. Don't be a networking stalker. Don't go about relentlessly pursuing a potential business associate or client who hasn't yet responded to your business or sales proposal. People don't fancy being hounded at networking events. If it looks like a contact isn't responding to your request, move on to more encouraging and receptive prospects/associates.

18. Keep it brief. When it comes to sharing your professional profile, keep it short by sticking to 2-3 sentences. Volunteer with the details only if someone asks for it later. Don't get into an elaborate presentation about your services. This is a guaranteed way to make people lose interest immediately. Don't fill your conversation with too many technical jargons. If

someone doesn't understand what you're saying, they will find it difficult to connect with you and your services.

19. Go with a goal. Before you attend a business event, make sure you know exactly why you're going there. Have clear goals. For instance, you may be looking to get a job lead or connect with five new company representatives or re-connecting with a few old business contacts. Whatever it is – make sure it's well-defined. Stay focused to your goal, and don't move around cluelessly at the event.

20. Read newspapers, even sections you aren't interested in. Devote a few minutes every morning to browsing the day's headlines, across multiple sections if possible. Even if you detest the sports section, go through it. People, especially men, often start conversations by discussing the previous night's games. If you can have a meaningful conversation about recent news items, you're less likely to feel left out.

21 Don't feel intimidated. Yes, we get it that you are in the midst of the most successful, inspiring and talented folks. However, that shouldn't break into cold sweat and feel any less about yourself. These are powerful people, but they are just people, like you. Of course, you have a lot to learn from them. That doesn't mean they have nothing to learn from you. Shine like you are meant to shine and stop feeling intimidated in the presence of stalwarts from your industry. It will show in the way you conduct yourself.

Chapter Twelve: Tips For Boosting Your Charisma as a Leader

We've all heard about people being charismatic leaders and communicators, and their unflinching ability to persuade or influence others. There are certain traits that the most popular boy in class or the life of a party or the most sought after CEO possess. Charisma is easy to spot but hard to define. It is the sort of thing that makes people appealing to others, and often comprises a set of characteristics like top-notch communication skills, ace leadership virtues and a sort of indescribable magnetism that draws people to them. These people are almost always positive, inspiring, great communicators and out of the ordinary.

However, if you don't identify yourself as a person with charisma, don't fret. It isn't something people are born with. Charisma or sound communication skills are something that can be developed with consistency, practice and a hands-on approach.

Being a leader, influencer or persuader isn't easy but it's not something that's an asset of a chosen few. It can be developed by anyone willing to give it a fair chance. Some people are naturally charismatic, while others have to put in more effort. This book will explore several strategies through which just about anyone can be more charismatic and an exceptionally good communicator.

Advantages of Being a Charismatic Leader

Articulation of Ideas

People understand your message loud and clear, and flock to your side when you have the ability to communicate your message is a convincing and compelling manner. It is easy to convey your vision to people when you are a splendid communicator. When you're able to explain complex issues with clarity and objectivity, it is easier to accomplish personal and professional goals.

More Fulfilling Interpersonal Relationships

Communication is often the only factor that makes or breaks personal relationships, which means it is even more important when it comes to interpersonal relationships. You must be able to delve into matters of importance and communicate personal feelings to your partner or even friends/family to be able to maintain a harmonious personal equation. Verbal and non-verbal communication both lead to more fulfilling relationships, where partners don't drift apart. Unlike popular perception, charisma works wonders even in personal relationships, and not just leadership roles.

Greater Professional Success

Imagine being able to negotiate your way through deals, a pay hike, greater responsibility and much more. Being a master communicator or charismatic communicator helps you become more productive, less stressed and more confident. It increases your social networking skills, helps you co-ordinate effectively with your team and leads the path for mutual trust.

Less Stress

When you learn to communicate more assertively and effectively, you learn to say no to unproductive things that sap your energy. You also eliminate the scope for misunderstandings, conflicts, misunderstandings and arguments. There is a greater ability to stay in control and manage uncomfortable situations around you. You develop better negotiation skills, and learn to be a persuader/influencer.

Think of all the times you've blurted out something in the heat of the moment, only to regret it later. Effective communicators are more adept at exercising self-control or avoiding impulsive actions. They know what to say, and how to say it for creating the desired impact.

Greater Understanding of Self

Along with helping to establish better connections with others, communication also helps you gain a greater understanding of yourself. Why do you feel the way you do when someone criticizes you? How can you overcome the anxiety/nervousness that takes over you when it comes to approaching your crush?

You gain a better understanding of your strengths and weaknesses by constantly interacting with others.

Tips For Growing Your Charisma

Marilyn Monroe asked a photographer to accompany her in New York City's Grand Central Station. There were people all around the place and no one recognized her as a Marylyn – the star, one of the world's most famous persons. She boarded and rode along to the subsequent station without so much as being noticed by anyone. Marilyn was Norma Jean (her real name) on the subway. However, once she was on New York's busy streets, she asked the photographer if he wanted to see Marilyn.

Just then, she left all guard and without any ostentatious gestures she puffed up her hair a bit and struck a magnificent pose. With one stroke of genius, she suddenly transformed into a star who that dazzled everyone around her. People just couldn't take their eyes off her.

Make no mistake there, she was gorgeous, but what there was a bigger point she was making. It is that charisma can be created, and radiated because it isn't just something one is born with.

Dig deep and there's a Marilyn Monroe underneath every Norma Jean Baker. One just needs to make an effort to find their inner star.

So how can one develop an irresistible persona or high charisma quotient? What is that mojo or charisma that separates the winners from the losers? That unexplainable "x" factor that destines one for success. Here are some cool ways to boost your charisma factor.

Confidence

Confidence is your magic potion for developing more charisma. It doesn't build overnight, and you don't have to come across as arrogant. However, being self-assured means being comfortable in your own skin, and maintain a certain posture while talking to people. Don't appear timid, intimated or overwhelmed.

Wear smart, well-fitting clothes that make you feel great about yourself because it invariably reflects in the way you carry yourself.

Speak confidently. This obviously doesn't mean talking louder or more than others. It is about saying the right and important things with the required panache/conviction. Speak clearly and with a more even pace. Keep changing the volume, tone, pitch and cadence frequently to keep the speech engaging and interesting. Practice talking with confidence. One of the best tips to develop more confidence is to stand in front of the mirror and speak, while observing your mannerisms, voice and body language when you speak. You can also record yourself while speaking, while hearing it later and noting down the changes that are needed to make the speech more impactful.

Remember, confidence is a constant work in progress, and it's tough to fake (though some people have indeed mastered the art). It is only when you genuinely feel confident from within that it reflects on your outer persona. If you don't feel good and confident from within, delve deep and try to figure out what's bothering you, and work on it. Highlight your positives, indentify and address your flaws, and focus on enhancing your skills and appearance if it makes you feel good.

A self-assured voice, neat clothes and confident body language goes a long way in creating your charisma.

Reveal Moral Conviction

Moral significance is another factor that makes you a more charismatic leader and communicator. When you appeal people to do the right thing, and lead by example, you automatically allow people to look up to you. There is a sense of shared values, inspiration and ability to urge stir others into take the right action.

During the MDNA tour Madonna sported a "pussy riot" on the back in support of imprisoned Russians. She was simply trying to create a sense of oneness and belongingness by attempting to show solidarity through righteousness. Doesn't this increase her charisma as an artist?

Set High Expectations

This holds true for yourself and others. Inspire those around you to push the envelope, and do their best. Set high expectations for others as well as yourself, and strive to accomplish it. Prince signed up and even produced The Time band for Warner Brothers. He urged everyone to enhance their stage shows.

According to the artists, Prince goaded everyone to sing and dance when they played. He brought about an element of positive change by teaching musicians to do things they thought were impossible. If you set elevated expectations for people, and help them realize their capability, your charisma automatically increases.

Use Lists and Facts

One of the best ways to boost charisma is by giving an impression of possessing a lot of knowledge, including facts and figures about multiple topics. People with extensive knowledge and information are instantly likeable. Lists reveal that you possess a coherent understanding about the issue you are addressing. The difference between charisma and the absence of it is often listing facts in a confident and coherent manner.

For instance, a person may say, "the new rules are going to affect us in many ways", while another may say, "The new rules are going to affect the staff in four significant ways such as..." Who do you think sounds more confident, coherent and self-assured? You instantly position yourself as someone in command of what he/she is speaking.

Part of being an engaging communicator and charismatic leader is the ability to charm different groups of people with proficiency in varied topics. Stay well-read, expose yourself to different sources of information and learn about different cultures. Knowledge of foreign languages, history of different regions, political situation in other countries and modern art almost always comes handy when talking to diverse groups. Well-rounded knowledge can be used to customize knowledge according to the person you're talking to.

Take time to think before speaking. Decrease fluff, and fillers while communicating. Make each word impactful. Phrase your words mentally instead of blurting them out randomly. If there's nothing worthwhile to say, stay silent. Restricting the amount you speak will make what you say more impactful and interesting.

Make People Feel Special

Charm every individual you meet by making them feel that they are really special. A truly charismatic person should be able to able to converse with or hold an arresting conversation with anyone based on their interests. Be an attentive listener who is always interested in what other people are feeling and speaking. People rarely forget the way you make them feel, and talking to them on an equal footing (font put them on elevated pedestal or talk down) makes them feel respected. This invariably increases your charisma quotient.

Show a deep interest in the lives of people without appearing nosy or judgmental. Express genuine interest in people's backgrounds, lives, opinions on matters that affect them and thoughts. It makes you instantly likeable and relatable. Always lend your ear to people who are expressing concern about something that deeply affects them. Value their thoughts and opinions, and make them feel that there's no way like them in the world. It goes a long way in increasing your charisma.

If you've read Dale Carnegie's path breaking book *How to Win Friends and Influence People* you'll realize that one of the things he had highlighted was remembering people's names and addressing them with it. This will show them that they were important enough for you to recollect details about them, which is wonderful charisma booster.

Another super way to make people feel special is by offering gracious and genuine compliments. Remember to not keep dropping compliments at every given instance. Keep them rare and genuine or people will quickly gather that you're compliments aren't sincere.

Be Witty

Wit and humor contributes hugely to your charisma. The most charismatic politicians, leaders, rock-stars and actors are those who have the ability to say the right things at the right time, and pepper their conversation with plenty of wit. There's a reason Oprah is one of the highest paid television personalities. She is a perfect blend of humor and empathy, tow traits that lead a charismatic persona.

Charm folks with your well-timed sense of humor, even when it comes to laughing at yourself. This makes you more comfortable, courageous and confident. Being able to indulge in self-deprecating humor is a sign of huge confidence, which automatically increases your charisma.

Laughter is one the best ways to establish your charisma. When you make your date or prospect laugh, it not just makes them comfortable but also makes them look forward to hearing more enjoyable conversations from you. Salespersons who make their potential customers laugh are almost always able to get them to buy. You know why the wittiest guys get the best girls, right?

Learn to sense the kind of humor a group enjoys and appreciates if you want to quickly boost your communicator or charisma quotient. Be attuned and sensitive to every person's sense of humor. Don't crack jokes that are offensive or in bad taste. It is alright if the group is raunchy, however you may need to tone to down when it comes to an older and more sensitive group.

When you meet people for the first time, take time to understand their idea of humor, how conservative they are and what classifies as appropriate or inappropriate for them.

Charismatic people don't try very hard to be hilarious. Also, you don't need to crack jokes every minute. Always let quality override quantity, and focus on drawing attention to your jokes by keeping them rare and well-timed.

Build a rapport by teasing and flirting with people one you establish a comfort level with them. People are easily taken in and charmed by those who teasingly have fun with them or reveal that they don't take things too personally or seriously. Just ensure that the jokes are cracked in the right spirit of things, and that people are not offended when you are playfully mocking them.

Be Positive

Well, this isn't just a blood group but an entire philosophy of life. Positive people are generally confident and encouraging. When you meet new people, don't start the conversation by being critical about a personal or political party or culture. Focus your energies instead on making a positive comment about something that engages people's attention. People love to be around positive folks. If they feel like there's only negativity and hate coming their way, they'll stay away from your to avoid the destructive vibe.

Smile gracefully and genuinely when you are introduced to someone for the first time. Your smile should reveal that you are truly enthusiastic or excited about being introduced to them.

Use Personal Anecdotes

Charismatic people almost always make themselves instantly likeable and relatable to any group by sharing personal stories. They try to establish a common ground with the group and make the conversation or speech more interesting and engaging. Paul McCartney uses this tactic brilliantly. Before introducing songs during his live performance, he gives a background story of it in terms of the inspiration behind the song or things that occurred during the making of the song.

Another great tip for being an engaging conversationalist is peppering your speech/talks with a lot of rhetorical questions. Is everyone here enjoying the show? It builds a sort of anticipation. Questions like "What next?" or "What will be our next move?" will have people latching on to every word.

Contrast also works well when you're trying to make a powerful point. Create contrasting statements that emphasize your point to make the point even more effective. Instead of simply saying, "we are concerned about the value our employees put in", say "While other organizations count hours, we are concerned about the value our employees create." It sounds more impactful and makes you come across as a master communicator.

Display Impactful Body Language

Nonverbal communication accounts for a staggering 80 percent of our communication, while only 20 percent can be attributed to verbal communication. Your body language makes you come across as confident, approachable and enthusiastic. Awkward body language, on the other hand, can make you appear shy, intimidated and indecisive.

Always stand tall and walk with an erect posture, taking steady yet resolute strides. Instead of crossing hands over the chest, use them to make animated gestures that make you come across as a more interesting conversationalist.

Enhance your posture. Sit straight with your head held high always, but don't appear rigid. When you are introducing yourself, never hesitate to offer a firm handshake and maintain eye contact. Always keep your body language positive, self-assured and approachable. Always face the person/people you're in conversation with. Avoid crossing arms and legs, and it's a huge sign that you aren't subconsciously open to what they are saying. It creates a sort of unspoken barrier, and puts people off.

Always appear in control and at ease. Avoid fidgeting or revealing obvious signs of nervousness. As mentioned in an earlier point, one of the best ways to practice improving your body language in standing and talking before a mirror. Watch your gestures, eye movements, expressions, posture etc. and identify areas that can be worked upon.

One of the best ways to get people to like you is to mimic their tone, postures, gestures, expressions and eye movements. It sends a message subconsciously that you are following what the other person in saying or validating their actions, which makes you more charismatic. Don't make the mirroring too obvious though otherwise the other person will misunderstand it as a means of mocking him/her.

Keep it more subtle like drinking a sip from your glass after they have lifted their glass to have a sip or using the same words/phrases that they use. This will make you more likeable, appealing and a master communicator.

Be Empathetic

People who are in touch with their inner emotions almost always appear more likeable to others. Their ability to process their and other's emotions helps people strongly relate to them, and increases their charisma quotient. When you display an ability to feel what others are feeling, it makes you come across as considerate and sensitive person. Don't be afraid to reveal elation, disappointment, hope, sorrow and other feelings in a suitable manner.

People end up hiding their true emotions and thoughts from others without any ulterior motives. However, opening up only warms people up to you. It makes you come across as honest and real, while also helping other people to open up for establishing a genuine rapport. A huge part of being a charmer is being genuine.

Master Presence

We all love speaking about ourselves. However, very few people have the ability to shut their egos, and give others an opportunity to talk about themselves, while listening to them with rapt attention.

Being mindful and attentive is a huge part of being a charismatic communicator. Invest your energy in listening to and focusing on others. Listen to people actively, and not to plan your next retort to what they're saying. Sometimes, we're so busy trying to frame our responses that we stop listening to the other person. Maintain a balance between talking and listening. Express yourself in a manner that doesn't make the other person feel like he/she is being talked down to.

People often misleading believe that developing charisma is all about waxing eloquence about their special qualities. Rather than trumpeting your virtues, help the other people feel wonderful about themselves. Genuine charisma is all about making others feel special and important than they did before interacting with you.

When you are communicating with other people, imagine you're reading a captivating book or watching a thrilling movie and you're just getting to know the protagonist. Give them complete attention as if an interesting story is unfolding before you. This alone makes you a more effective and charismatic communicator.

Notice how some people always look preoccupied or checking their phones when you talk to them? Isn't this a huge turn off? Listen mindfully when others are conversing with you. Give them undivided attention, and refrain from focusing on anything else during the moment. It's your opportunity to connect with people, make the most of it. The gift of absolute and undivided attention will always be remembered by people, thus making you a charismatic communicator.

Offer a Useful Takeaway

Whether you are addressing a group or talking to an individual, always help them return with at least one powerful actionable tip. This is especially true for people who are struggling with an issue. Rather than pitying them or offering unsolicited sermons about how they should lead their life, begin by empathizing with them.

Next, present a few actionable solutions that can be implemented almost immediately. People value advice that is practical and doable. For instance, is a person is suffering from a binge eating condition, rather than giving them lectures about healthy eating, suggest some quick remedies while also asking them to see a medical practitioner.

Adapt to Different Communication Styles

If you're the leader of an organization or soon assuming a leadership role (holds good even in your personal life), you have to embrace differences and quickly adapt to multiple communication styles. For instance, if you are managing personnel across several age groups, you have to adopt a communication style that is distinct to them.

For instance, older coworkers will have a different style of communication than Gen-Y millenials. The former may prefer face to face communication, while the later will ask for real time updates and communication via instant messaging applications.

If you're in a leadership role, you'll obviously set the team communication rhythm. However, you'll also have to be mindful of differences.

Manage Your Expectations

Managing your own expectations is critical to avoiding feelings of resentment, bitterness and anger. When it doubt – always play it cool. Try and focus on what the other is trying to convey.

Avoid letting your expectations soar at the onset. When we are about to meet people for the first time or communicate about an important issue, our inability to manage our lofty expectations creates a huge potential for disappointment.

This invariably leads to us holding grudges against people, getting hurt and becoming angry. Hurt feelings may not lead to effective communication in future or may hamper the rapport building process. The best way to avoid these destructive emotions is to acquire the art of minding your own expectations.

You know what's the best attitude? Always ensure the person walks out of the room feeling way better than he did about himself/herself when he/she walked in. That is the sign for a master communicator.

Good communicators always set limits for curbing arguments and hostility. When you get a feel that the talk can quickly escalate into a full-blown argument, get into action and establish limits. Say things like, "Oh! I never really thought of it from this perspective" or "your point may indeed have some substance." This gives the impression that you aren't closed to the other person's perspective, and that you respect it. Agreeing to disagree harmoniously is one of the biggest traits of a master communicator, which will help you build harmonious and fulfilling relationships in future.

Conclusion

Thank you for purchasing this book.

I hope it was able to help you achieve a deeper understanding of leadership in an engaging and enjoyable manner.

The next step is to simply implement the nuggets of wisdom, actionable steps and practical tips described in this valuable resource.

Finally, if you enjoyed reading the book, please take the time to share your thoughts and post a review. It'd be greatly appreciated!

www.ingramcontent.com/pod-product-compliance
Lightning Source LLC
Chambersburg PA
CBHW070652220526
45466CB00001B/405